"Dr. Jennifer Turner has written another encouraging, challenging, and practical book. The reader is encouraged to turn to the scriptures to clearly see the loving character of God. We are gently challenged to examine our own relationship with our good Heavenly Father and the life experiences that have impacted that relationship. Through the sharing of personal experiences of her journey with God, Dr. Turner brings a warmth and reality to following Jesus in the power of the Holy Spirit. This is a must read for all those who long for a deeper understanding of God's love."

—Jackie Stoneman, Former Principal, Mary Andrews College, Sydney

"If you want more from your relationship with God, sit back, relax, and enjoy reading *Home with the Good Father*. Dr Turner's wisdom, experiences, and caring style will help you to appreciate our Father's love in fresh ways."

—Stephen Parker, Associate Professor for Pastoral Theology, Australian College of Ministries

"Jennifer writes as one with personal knowledge of the 'Good Father,' and this book is her way of communicating that experience to us. She invites us into a richer and deeper experience of God as we 'come home' and are graciously welcomed—no matter where we have been or what we have done. Blending storytelling and theological reflection, she helps us find the path to the kind of relationship we hope to have with our Father God."

—Andrew Hamilton, author of *The Future is Bivocational: Shaping Christian Leaders for a Post-Christian World*

"We are all searching for home. Jennifer Turner understands this, and in her wonderful book, *Home with the Good Father*, she gently points us towards paths that lead to deeper intimacy with God. Using motifs from the parable of the prodigal son(s) and supplementing them with relatable stories from her life, she helps us explore blocks we might face in our journey. This is a deeply encouraging book, written for all with a longing for home."

—Brian Harris, Former Principal, Vose Seminary

Home with the Good Father

Home with the Good Father

Living in God's Abundant Love

JENNIFER TURNER

Foreword by Graham Joseph Hill

WIPF & STOCK · Eugene, Oregon

HOME WITH THE GOOD FATHER
Living in God's Abundant Love

Wipf & Stock
An Imprint of Wipf and Stock Publishers
199 W. 8th Ave., Suite 3
Eugene, OR 97401

www.wipfandstock.com

PAPERBACK ISBN: 979-8-3852-6796-5
HARDCOVER ISBN: 979-8-3852-6797-2
EBOOK ISBN: 979-8-3852-6798-9

VERSION NUMBER 04/28/26

For the great men in my life:
Neil and our sons Matthew, Calvin, and Kirk.

Contents

Foreword

There's a miracle at the heart of this book; one that unfolds gently, without spectacle, yet with the kind of strength that reshapes a life from the inside out. It's the miracle of coming home, not to a place, nor to an idea, but to the One who has been waiting with open arms since the first moment we dared to long for something more.

In these pages, you'll hear stories of weary travelers (some bold wanderers, some faithful plodders) learning again what it means to be welcomed, healed, delighted in, and sent back into the world with renewed courage. You'll hear of the prodigal whose shame seemed beyond repair and the older sibling whose resentment kept them outside the celebration. You'll hear of the seeker who tries not to ask too much, the one who fears their hurt is too deep, the one who longs for rescue but doubts they deserve it, the one who discovers awe in the everyday, and the one who has forgotten that grace is for them too.

These aren't abstract reflections. They come wrapped in real stories: Africa's danger and deliverance, the gut-level truth of shame and scars, the fragile beauty of asking prayer, the wonder of mountains and sunsets, the deep ache of loneliness, the relief of adoption, the companionship of the Spirit, and the steady, transforming presence of Jesus who, astonishingly, comes to dwell in the house with us.

What strikes me most as I read this book is the way it balances tenderness and truth. The writer doesn't hurry past the hard things. There are wounds here, disappointments, seasons of confusion, hesitations about prayer, resistance to grace, and the subtle pride that keeps many of us dutifully working in the fields. At the same time, the music of celebration drifts from the house. Yet resounding through every chapter is a profound conviction: that our frailty, our ambivalence, or our unfinished stories don't scandalize the Good Father. Instead, God meets us where we are: welcoming the runaway, pleading with the resentful, comforting the ashamed, steadying the fearful, and inviting all of us into a life marked by intimacy, awe, joy, and deep belonging.

This book is a gentle guide for anyone who has ever wondered whether God truly wants them. It's a steadying companion for those learning to pray with trust, to walk through healing with courage, and to receive love without defensiveness. It's a prophetic nudge to those of us who hide behind competence or duty. And it's a reminder that the Christian life is not a matter of gritting our teeth and trying harder but of allowing ourselves to be caught up in the love that's been pursuing us from the beginning.

You hold in your hands an invitation, not to analyze a parable but to step inside it. Not to perform for God but to rest in God. Not to strive toward an imagined holiness but to receive the life of the Son through the Spirit who forms us into a family likeness we can never achieve on our own.

May you hear, as you read, the Father's voice whispering your name. May you find yourself turning toward the house where the lights are on, the table is set, and the celebration has already begun. May you dare to believe that this welcome is for you.

GRAHAM JOSEPH HILL, OAM, PHD
Sydney, Australia

Acknowledgments

There are many people who have contributed to my life and to this book. It has been so important to be part of a faith community, and especially to share in a small group where we often "riff" into all manner of topics as well as tell our stories. Some of these are recorded in these chapters with my gratitude. I particularly thank Briallen, Ann, and Sace for their accounts of hearing God's voice at crucial times in their lives and Ray Forlin whose work on the biblical understanding of adoption introduced me to this wonderful truth. Chris and Aimee Ingram have been valuable supporters.

Others have contributed by reading the chapters as I wrote them. To Ailsa and Ann and Jo I say a big *thank you*. Each of you brought a different perspective which widened my thinking as well as encouraged me to continue refining the words I was using.

My husband, Neil, again read the text with ready red pen in hand and provided a scientist's viewpoint that balanced my cultural and social approach. One of the best things we have shared through more than fifty years of marriage is our love of the Scriptures, and I have greatly appreciated his God-given insights, particularly when daily we are reading the same passage but approaching it from our different backgrounds and interests.

Thank you too to Graham Joseph Hill for his readiness to introduce this book through writing the foreword and to those churches and groups who have invited me to speak, trusting me to faithfully handle God's word and tell the good news of divine love seen in Jesus.

Finally, my gratitude to Elissa who first said of the Good Father, "Remember who is inviting you into his presence!"

Invitation

Are you satisfied with your life?

Does anyone ever answer "Yes!" to that?

There *are* times when things seem to be going right. Maybe we feel fulfilled if we have just completed a particularly rewarding task, or a much longed-for child has arrived safely, or we have moved into a promising new job or house. Or perhaps when friends have gone home after an evening spent together, and we are basking in the lingering warmth of respect and enjoyment of each other, we have a sense of real contentment.

But if, in that afterglow, we are asked to rate our satisfaction level, we know that there are plenty of other corners of our life where we long for more. Yet we have a sneaking suspicion that we should not be expecting more. In fact, we may even feel we do not deserve what we have now! So we settle for less than all we might have or be. And we give up our search for unconditional love.

Most of the time we do not even dare to acknowledge our appetite for more. We do not want to be disappointed or greedy. Sure, when the going is tough, we think it is not fair that we must struggle on, but we manage to keep our heads above water, making gradual improvements until things are on an even keel again. Then we settle once more for normal. "She'll be right, mate!" we might say in the Australian way.

There are always a few who strive for excellence—the athlete, the business highflyer, the talented craftswoman or man. We grudgingly admire their persistence, their rewards. We also wish these high achievers were more like the rest of us. And if we do not go so far as to cut down the tall poppies, we certainly make clear to ourselves and others that we are not as fanatical as they are.

We settle for less than the best in our relationship with God too. We tell ourselves that absence of pain, an even keel, a general sense that we are accepted, is all we need. We dare not acknowledge our hunger for more spiritually, or that our relationship with God is not totally satisfying. But there is much more! God has so much more for us to experience, more to know, more to grow, more love. C. S. Lewis put this well:

> If we consider the unblushing promises of reward and the staggering nature of the rewards promised in the Gospels, it would seem our Lord finds our desires, not too strong, but too weak. We are half-hearted creatures, fooling about with drink and sex and ambition when infinite joy is offered us, like an ignorant child who wants to go on making mud pies in a slum because he cannot imagine what is meant by the offer of a holiday at the sea. We are too easily pleased.[1]

Does this describe you? Are you too easily pleased spiritually? Or are you ready for more? The deepening Christian life that God offers us is there for the seeking—if we do not settle for too little.

But perhaps you are afraid that if you seek more you will need to be a spiritual athlete, your whole life given over to rigorous discipline. Or be an unpopular fanatic who stands out like a sore thumb. Or that searching for more in your relationship with God will deny who you are as a person, renouncing *normal* life as you know it—something for the dedicated ascetic, the desert father, or the cloistered nun, but not for the ordinary twenty-first-century person trying to make ends meet, hold down a job, run a household, and raise the kids.

Hungering to know God better, to have the divine wholeness, power, and love flow through everyday life, does not come through retirement *from* everyday life, *from* the use of your mind, *from* the enjoyment of the physical life. Nor does pursuing God necessarily mean long hours of prayer in desert-like solitude, or foregoing engagement in a life of service.

I want to tell you there is more that God, the good Father, longs to give to his children. Starting from the story Jesus told about the prodigal son coming home to his father, this book is what I have discovered about receiving *all* God wants to give.

It is not a choice between *mind* or *feelings*, or between *spiritual* or *physical*. There is so much more that can enrich all we are as whole people in a real world. Our hunger for more, even though we may be suspicious of it, may be a loving God prodding us to search for, to ask for, that *more* that is available through Jesus. Dickens's Oliver Twist got into trouble for asking

1. Quoted in Piper, *Desiring God*, 77–78.

for more, but God does not come down heavily on Oliver Twists. Our Creator wants us to ask for more. Are you ready for that? More is available when you come home to God *the Good Father*—home where you belong!

1

Coming Home

The ultimate secret of this story is this: There is a homecoming for us all because there is a home.

—Helmut Thielicke, *The Waiting Father*

Jon Sanders piloted his little boat *Parry Endeavour* three times around the world without once putting in to shore. When finally, after nearly two years away, he sailed into his Australian home port, it was just as the world's eyes were on us here in Perth, hosting the America's Cup yachting classic. The people of our city turned out in force to welcome Jon Sanders home. Many were simply proud of his single-handed achievement. Others were caught up in the great drama that sailing presents. But the comments of people watching for him at the port that day showed that most stood in the bright sunshine and watched the boat approach land because they identified with the overwhelming joy of *coming home*—to safety and security, a dry bed, and a good meal.

Coming home! What a wonderful feeling! For all the adventures the world offers, home is where you are meant to be! We ordinary mortals will never know what it is like to be alone for as long as Jon Sanders was, facing icebergs at the tip of South America or fierce storms crossing the Indian Ocean, yet coming through with flying colors. And whether we have a home or not, we know what it is like to long for it. Home is where we can finally relax, be safe, and let down our mask. Home is where we expect to be seen and loved, wanted and understood. It is where we can care and give without being misunderstood.

THE JOY OF COMING HOME

One time I was talking with a prominent Australian scientist about the joys of returning home to Australia. At frequent intervals he was called overseas to contribute to the fast-moving field of molecular genetics. Whenever he wished, he could take up residence in California and lead his colleagues in worldwide research and development without the frustrations of budget contractions and the failure of nerve that seemed to characterize the local scientific endeavor. But still he kept coming back. "Why is it so comfortable to come home?" he asked.

We decided it was the accent. Not the accent itself but what it symbolizes. And not other people's accents but our own. I remember the first time I spent an extended period overseas. I had been warned by more experienced travelers that hearing Australians again in a raucous group would be a shock. I got that shock from a bunch of "ugly" Australian tourists in Singapore before I ever got to these familiar shores and jokingly said I should foreswear Australia forever!

But even though I am of the generation that was trained out of a broad Australian accent in the interests of middle-class respectability, I soon forget the harshness of Australian voices once I am back home. It is my own accent that does it. It reassures me that I fit in.

In the sixties we lived in the United States for seven years. We were doing work that was appreciated and well rewarded, but I always knew that whenever I opened my mouth, I gave away the fact that I was not an American. In many fields that would not matter. It does not matter now to my English husband that he will never sound like a local here in Australia. But I was a planning consultant, employed to help people discover how to live best in their piece of America, in their town. If they did not like the advice they were getting, they could hear my accent and call me a foreigner and ask what right I had to interfere with "The American Way."

Even worse, after I had addressed a public meeting on some portentous issue such as new state legislation for the preservation of wetlands, folks would come up to me and say how much they liked my *accent*. Apparently, they had not heard *what* I had to say about saving wetlands, only *how* I said it! I was a novelty. I did not really belong.

HOME IS THE PLACE WHERE YOU BELONG

Home is where you belong. It is where you kick off your shoes and feel comfortable. These are comforts you only really appreciate when you do not have them—like the Australian affection for vegemite or the gray green of gum leaves or the smell of first rain on red dirt when you are overseas and have not experienced them for a while. On a recent return home, my husband noticed that it was the chiming of the clock he inherited from his grandmother, now installed in the entrance foyer of our house, which helped him feel at home. *His* home.

C. S. Lewis writes of loving home as a precursor of affection. He says it can be the first welcome step away from the tyranny of a self-love that wants only to maintain itself. This love of home is a good thing—though not the kind of nationalism that extols *our* way as the *only* way, forcing it on others. He quotes the Greeks, "No man loves his city because it is great, but because it is his."[1] It is like the affection for the past that expresses itself in the childhood songs and hymns we continue to hum, though we might reject both their trite theology and their rhythms. They are part of the comfort of where we have come from, a reminder of years of acceptance and belonging.

American poet Robert Frost (1874–1963) pictures home in similar terms. In his enigmatic work "The Death of the Hired Hand," the old weak farmworker Silas comes back to die after earlier abandoning his family. The wife takes him in, despite her husband's uncertainty and self-doubt about his right to ask it of her. He finally consoles himself with the words, "'Home is the place where, when you have to go there, they have to take you in.' But his long-suffering wife put it better: 'I should have called it something you somehow haven't to deserve.'"[2]

In her recent novel about homecoming, Australian author Kate Morton's character, twenty-something Jess, experiences the loneliness of leaving home to live in faraway London. Even after years of exciting work there and finding an English partner, it is the pull of home that draws her back in a surprising return to Sydney, still searching for, in T. S. Eliot's phrase, "the still point of the turning world."

> Home, she'd realised, wasn't a place or a time or a person, though it could be any and all of those things: home was a feeling, a sense

1. Lewis, *Four Loves*, 30.
2. Quoted in Stevens, *Equipper's Guide*, 132.

> of being complete. The opposite of "home" wasn't "away," it was "lonely." When someone said, "I want to go home," what they really meant was that they didn't want to feel lonely anymore.[3]

Psychologist Paul Tournier writes of the psychological need for "place" out of his own experience of losing both his parents at a young age. He describes the importance of belonging and being known, of overcoming loneliness in terms of home. He quotes a client: "Basically I have always been looking for a place. A place to call home."[4] Town planners now speak of "place" in a city or town as having all the qualities of rounded community life, a place not vacant but peopled.

WHEN HOME IS NOT WHAT IT SHOULD BE

The ideal of home is not always our experience, however. Not all of us find home (or country or place) to be like that. Home can also be a place of emotional emptiness, even abuse and insecurity. In fact, the kind of evil our society has become increasingly concerned about is *domestic* violence, in the home.

Later in Morton's *Homecoming* novel, Jess finds an ancestral home in the Adelaide Hills, not Sydney, and it has an even greater psychological pull on her, but it is associated with a great tragedy. The police sergeant investigating multiple murders at the abandoned house explains the focus of his investigation:

> It was one of the oldest rules in the policing handbook; in the case of sudden death, look first to the next of kin. For all that "home" was considered a word of warmth and comfort, policemen knew better. Home is where the heart is, and the heart could be a dark and damaged place.[5]

The very fact that we feel cheated if we are not safe, accepted and loved at home, indicates how profound are our expectations that there should be somewhere in this world where we belong, some "still point" where we are seen and appreciated. Its absence can be devastating. Accent or experience or relationship may assure us that this is where we ought to belong, but our hearts or bruises sometimes tell us the reality is otherwise.

3. Morton, *Homecoming*, 587.
4. Tournier, *Place for You*, 9.
5. Morton, *Homecoming*, 377.

THE PRODIGAL COMES HOME

Jesus, the supreme storyteller, also told a tale about coming home, one that has resonated down the centuries. It begins,

> There was a man who had two sons. The younger one said to his father, "Father, give me my share of the estate." So he divided his property between them. Not long after that, the younger son got together all he had, set off for a distant country and there squandered his wealth in wild living. (Luke 15:11–13)

The young man in Jesus' story tries everything he can think of in his quest for adventure, but when he has run through all his money and friends, and a famine threatens his very survival, he gets as low as eating scraps meant for pigs. So he decides it is time to go home. Leaving those many months before, he had demanded his share of the family inheritance to fund his journey, and he has no reason to expect a warm welcome back from the old man. All the way home he rehearses the speech he never got to make. "Just take me back in," he would say. "I don't deserve to simply slip again into all the privileges of a son. I know I've squandered the family assets. Just let me live in the house and do the work."

But as he trudges the last few miles down the road feeling sorry for himself and comes in sight of the family home, there is his father out looking for him. No doubt about the warmth of the welcome he gets. The father would hear none of this "make me like one of your hired servants." The son was well and truly to be part of the family again. And never mind that the older brother does not think it was fair that the prodigal[6] gets all the home privileges back. His harsh reaction only shows how unexpected and generous their dad is—that even a wandering son can again access home and all that being part of a family means. Moreover, as if being home and accepted back is not enough, his father lays on a celebration party and publicly announces how glad he is to have the wayward son back, despite the shame he has brought on the family.

What if the younger son had said, "I've done my dash. No chance of going back. I've lost my home forever"? He would never have known the warmth of the welcome waiting for him. Even when he got there, if he had

6. Though it is not a word he used, in Jesus' story *prodigal* is commonly understood to mean the younger son was *wayward*. I am following that common usage to distinguish him from his older brother. Some, however, use *prodigal* of the father in this story, because his *recklessly extravagant* love is closer to its dictionary meaning.

crawled into the attic and lived in the house as a servant or guest, he would have missed out on so much that his father was glad to give him.

WE LONG FOR HOME TOO

We often find ourselves searching for something more in life, that more that *home* represents, a place where we are accepted. We need to hear this prodigal story reminding us that God is out looking for us, initiating contact and inviting us *home*. God is the host ushering us into safety and security because the world is not always benign. We need shelter, protection, a home.

Psalmist David knew this when surrounded by wild animals and wild people:

> My choice is you, GOD, first and only.
> And now I find I'm your choice!
> You set me up with a house and a yard.
> And then you made me your heir!
> (Ps 16:5–6 MSG)

And from one of his other familiar psalms, "Your mercy and love chase after me every day of my life" (Ps 23:6 MSG).

COMING HOME TO GOD

The prodigal's return is the picture Jesus gives us of coming home to God. Through it, he invites us to our most significant *coming home*. We may feel alienated and alone in the universe, experiencing rejection by those who should love and protect us. We may have despaired of ever being acceptable to someone we value. Then grace *dawns* on us, catches us unawares. God's grace—that unexpected and unearned acceptance—comes generously to us through Jesus. *Dawns* seems the best word to describe it because it is much more than a mind thing; it is felt in our inner being, in our heart. It *dawns* through our awareness that we are indeed loved and lovable. It was what the prodigal experienced when he saw his father, out of the house, welcoming him back home.

Maybe previously you have known something of the generous acceptance and love God offers through Jesus. But you now find yourself trying to manage life on your own, in your own way. But a crisis or a loss, a new responsibility like the birth of a child, or a reassessment of priorities in midlife, is bringing you back home.

Others of you, having rejected a secondhand spirituality absorbed through your family, now want to own faith for yourself as an adult by coming back home to God by choice. You want to feel the undeserved welcome personally, in your own experience.

In a different way, Ruth Haley Barton applies *homecoming* to her movement back into a newly rich relationship with God through the church.[7] As a woman who had always valued her Christian community, she had found nevertheless that her church did not value her. Their rejection conflicted with the heart and gifts she realized she had been given, and it greatly pained her. But when she made space in her life to finally hear what God thought of her as a woman, her homecoming was to both God and to a church that welcomed her and the gifts she brought to it.

Most wonderfully, however, you may be someone hearing for the first time the incredible news that God, this great Creator God, is not angry with you but really loves you and has made a way for you to find a home in a world that once felt empty and cold, a godless cosmos. You recognize that this is the love you have been looking for all your life, and you relax into God's acceptance, acknowledging the "amazing grace" offered to you, whatever your history.

HOME MEANS MORE THAN FOOD AND SHELTER

For those sorely in need of them, a *house* offers shelter (and presumably food) as the immediate priority. Refugees, street people, and others destitute through circumstances know only too well how essential it is to have somewhere to live. It is hard to manage life when this basic necessity is absent. Reliable shelter provides the safety and security essential to facing whatever next is coming your way. But a house is not a home. A roof over your head does not guarantee satisfactory relationships nor acceptance of your very existence. And if the food or shelter are given grudgingly, or must be slaved for, the manner of their giving diminishes their value to you.

In his novel *Lola in the Mirror*, Australian writer Trent Dalton's main character always insists she is not *homeless* but *houseless*.[8] She may spend her nights in a wrecked car on the banks of Queensland's Brisbane River,

7. See Johnson, *How I Changed My Mind*, 46.

8. Dalton, *Lola in the Mirror*.

but it is her *home*. It is surrounded by a community of car-dwelling *houseless* people, but they, too, are not *homeless*. Lola knows that despite their diversity and their extreme situation, they provide the benefits, the acceptance, and the love for each other expected of *home*. Home is more than four walls; it represents more intangible benefits.

Acceptance is the first gift of really being home, of being welcomed through the door. The prodigal younger son in Jesus' story was thinking about food when sitting among the pigs and eating their scraps, and he was prepared to risk rejection to get at least something for his hunger and a roof over his head. But we know that his father's acceptance will be what matters most to him after that first meal.

This is what we, too, want most deeply, the kind of welcome that accepts who we are. Jesus' story has a little detail we may miss. "While he was still a long way off, his father saw him and was filled with compassion for him; *he ran to his son*, threw his arms around him and kissed him" (Luke 15:20; emphasis added). The welcome home the father offered him was the most wonderful acceptance and forgiveness.

AN UNEXPECTED WELCOME HOME

"Ran to his son"? Jesus lived in an honor-shame society, and his stories reflect this understanding of how his culture works. Each member of a household is expected to know their place and perform their role, never ever bringing shame on the family. Moreover, good order requires them to give the father respect and unchallenged obedience. Such a father would not normally be so undignified as to run and publicly welcome home an errant son. The renegade young man has broken all the rules. Not only has he caused financial hardship for his family by demanding an early share of his inheritance but he has brought dishonor on them and especially on his father by his disobedience and lack of respect. For the sake of the family's honor, the father is expected to shun him, certainly not give him back his place at home.

We will look in another chapter at the older son's reaction to the grace the younger son receives from his father. The "good" older brother's anger is a typical honor-shame reaction to what the prodigal has done to their family. Yet this father ignores that harsh expectation. Jesus paints a wonderful word picture of a dignified Middle Eastern patriarch surprisingly hitching up his robe and *running* to meet his son. What a welcome! What acceptance! What implied forgiveness! It would have been a shock to the older son.

THE DEMANDS OF AN HONOR-SHAME CULTURE

It is hard for Westerners who value individual expression and freedom of action to feel the weight that family honor imposes in this kind of honor-shame culture, or to comprehend the distance it puts between the "higher" and the "lower" members of a family or society. In recent years I have worked with students in South Asian cultures struggling under the negative impacts of such cultural expectations. These students find it very moving to see in the Gospel narratives the revolutionary way Jesus interacts with low-status people in his society—with the poor, women, lepers, outcasts, Samaritans. He treats them as equals with respect and worth, sometimes deliberately challenging existing patronizing attitudes.

But within Jesus' two-sons story, set in a typical scenario of his day and time, we are meant to be surprised by the love and forgiveness the father shows towards his returning son. It was certainly not what his hearers thought the prodigal deserved.[9]

Accompanying my husband on his visiting scientist sabbatical to the Philippines gave me my first personal encounter with the distancing honor-shame culture can bring to personal relationships. The housing we were offered for our stay came with servant's quarters. The expectation was that we would hire a maid to provide local employment and help in running the household. But we never became accustomed to having a servant. Australians of all people are uncomfortable with status hierarchy, so this was an intensive learning experience for all our family.

Sunday was our maid's day off to do as she pleased, to stay in or go out. She mostly chose to stay in, saying she had no family nearby. So early on, in our naivety, we invited her to sit down with us each week for our usual Sunday midday meal. She declined. We made it clear she did not have to prepare it or wait on us because it was her day off, but still she said no. Puzzled, we began to understand the social gulf an honor-shame culture perpetuates. Sitting down with the employer's family was a step too far, too uncomfortable for her, and we abandoned any effort to persuade her otherwise.

9. All cultures have their positives as well as their negatives. I do not mean to imply a condemnation of honor-shame societies, nor an uncritical endorsement of individualistic Western culture. I address the negatives of Western culture in chapter 6.

FORGIVENESS IS OFFERED

Jesus makes it clear in his story that the son did not expect anything but the most basic charity from his father.

> When he [the younger son] came to his senses, he said, "How many of my father's hired servants have food to spare, and here I am starving to death! I will set out and go back to my father and say to him: Father, I have sinned against heaven and against you. I am no longer worthy to be your son; make me like one of your hired servants." So he got up and went to his father.
>
> But while he was still a long way off, his father saw him and was filled with compassion for him; he ran to his son, threw his arms around him and kissed him.
>
> The son said to him, "Father, I have sinned against heaven and against you. I am no longer worthy to be called your son." (Luke 15:17–21)

The prodigal in the pigsty making the decision to return home did not expect to be forgiven and accepted back with such generosity. He was just desperate to at least get food and shelter, but the father offered him so much more. Had he not taken the step to turn around, to repent ("turn around" is what repenting means), he would have continued to live with the shame, the sense of unworthiness, of being alone, forever alienated, even if he had somehow gotten the food and shelter he needed.

But with the first sign of turning, he receives his father's acceptance, his forgiveness. The prodigal did not earn either acceptance or forgiveness by his turning. The father was ready to give them. His open arms promised that. But they would not have been available if he had not come home.

REBELS AND FAILURES

Later we will see how Jesus portrayed the older son in this story. The narrative ends with this older son still resisting his father's invitation to come in and receive all that was rightfully his. But no repenting, no forgiveness. John Stott has said, "Before God we are both rebels and failures."[10] The prodigal knows failure; the older son is a rebel. We all are one or the other, or both.

To come home to God, to experience all that is available, requires us to acknowledge we are not worthy; we have fallen short of our own

10. Stott, *Ephesians*, 71.

expectations of ourselves, let alone of our Creator's. Most of us know this deep down. Theologian and pastor Timothy Keller often put it in these words: "We are more flawed and sinful than you'd ever dare believe, and yet more loved and accepted than you'd ever dared hope—at the same moment."[11] David Benner, a psychologist, says it in his way: "Complete knowing of our self in relation to God includes three things: our self as deeply loved, our self as deeply sinful, and our self as in a process of being redeemed and restored."[12]

None of us deserve this generosity, this grace. None of us can claim a right to be treated differently than our actions deserve, to have a place back home with our name on the door. But repenting does not earn this generosity. God's nature is loving and forgiving, so our sinning hurts God's heart as much as ours. But the divine Father stands ready to forgive. We turn to bring ourselves into the place where we can receive the grace of forgiveness.

However, we are so determined to be independent that giving up any attempt to manage ourselves and our life feels like failure for most contemporary people. But we will not discover the acceptance and love we seek until we come to our senses, head for home, and find Father God is already out on the porch, looking for us with open arms.

Turning was the prodigal's act of repentance. So it is for us. God's desire to forgive is there before we turn. Our coming back does not earn it. Rather, we enter into it through the open arms of love because we are wanted and seen. Grace comes first—grace calling us through our longing for home.

How do we come to a realization of this grace? How do we experience it? It never ceases to surprise me the different ways God calls people home to love. One woman told me that when she was finding it difficult to believe God wanted her after the messy life she had led, a little bird came and sat on her windowsill each morning and seemed to her to chirp incessantly, "God loves you! God loves you!" She surrendered to that love.

GOD'S GENEROSITY SEEN

Like the father's welcome to his sons, God's forgiving generosity can be captured by other stories of grace. One writer puts this two-son parable in the contemporary dress of a young woman running away from a small-town

11. Keller, *Preaching*, 78.

12. Benner, *Gift of Being Yourself*, 67.

home only to get lost in prostitution, drugs, and finally poverty in a big, anonymous city. When she arrives at rock bottom, in desperation she messages home and fearfully and tentatively boards a bus back, daring to hope she will find her parents at the bus station welcoming her back with the open arms of grace. And she does. Her story ends in immense joy and celebration that someone once lost is now found.

Sometimes I, too, retell the prodigal story, placing it in the local cultural setting wherever I am. Rarely do I get to that final welcome home embrace without tears. I feel in my own life God's grace surrounding me and know again the immense joy and relief that is available for all. It seems that God's generosity in Jesus must not only be understood in our heads or even felt emotionally. Somehow both head and heart must come together so that we experience love and acceptance in the depths of our being.

Such grace is as much a necessity of life as food and shelter. It is needed not just once but time and time again when we fail trying to manage on our own. God is not surprised by our failing, though the divine Father is grieved. The wonder is that the arms are always open to love and love again, because even when we fall, we are never further from God's grace than the first time God urged us to come home. I cannot manufacture that awareness in you by retelling this story. It is the work of the Holy Spirit to bring you home to a loving Father who is waiting for you.

Maybe the words *father* and *home* bring a world of pain to you because of the treatment you received growing up at the hands of your earthly father. Maybe your home was far from happy, not the ideal place of acceptance pictured here. In the next chapter I tell the story of an abused young woman I have called "Jane" whose experience taught me that she, too, could experience the healing of coming home to a loving, safe, divine Father whom she could learn to call her *Good Father*.

RESPONDING

- In coming to faith, C. S. Lewis experienced God as "the hound of heaven," an expression used by Francis Thompson in his 1890 poem of that name. Does this resonate with you? Have you experienced God chasing after you?
- Later Lewis wrote of being *surprised* by the joy of being found by God. Was that your experience too? Did you welcome being found,

thinking it a surprising joy? What does it feel like for you to be accepted unconditionally? Ponder Romans 8:38–39.

- Do you find yourself coming back time and time again to God to ask for grace? However unworthy you feel, take comfort that God's mercy arises from *God's* character, not *yours*. This Father is reliable and constant, not changing like shifting shadows. There is nothing, either good or bad, that can rob you of God's unconditional love. Read 1 John 4:10 and give thanks.

2

An Incredible Intimacy

The most authentic and intense desires can be completed only in relation to God. The same God who created appetites in us also created the means to their satisfaction.

—Eugene Peterson, commenting on Psalm 63:5: "My soul is satisfied with a rich feast"

One evening we were sitting in one of those special little restaurants that overlook the Swan River in Perth. We could see the lights of a day/night game at the Western Australian Cricket Association ground (WACA) across the water as the towers of St Georges Terrace, which mark the business heart of Perth, were fading into darkness. A visiting professor my husband was working with had taken us out to dinner at the end of his week's stay. Finally, he voiced the question that I had seen on his face several times that week. "You people are Christians. What does God mean to people like you?"[1]

I said something about experiencing a personal relationship with the God of the universe.

Then I stopped as I heard what I had just said. How preposterous a claim that is! A personal relationship? With one who by very definition is so far beyond and above us? But that is what I believe. That is what I

1. I first told this story in Turner, "Hunger for Intimacy."

experience. That is what I have seen change, heal, and revitalize those who come home to God.

I watched to see his reaction. His face clouded over. We went on to talk in theoretical terms about the intimacy we hope for in all our relationships and the hunger we experience when it is not there. And then he told us about his Welsh mother.

She had been an active Christian, but when he was only a child, she died on a visit to Australia in connection with some Christian endeavor which he barely understood. But what he did understand was that he had been robbed of his precious mother, of what should be his innate right to her love and protection. It seemed to him that her relationship with God had not prevented her premature death, indeed it had caused it. His current trip to Australia was in part to revisit that pain, find an explanation and perhaps healing. Inevitably for him as a scientist it was also linked to his search for meaning behind the science in which he was a recognized authority.

There are many links between our human search for intimacy and our hunger for God. It is very difficult for hurting men or women to accept that the God of the universe is favorably disposed toward them, especially those who have not known an affectionate and protective human parent. That is why Jesus' portrayal of God as a father is so poignant. The father's welcome home to his straying son in the prodigal story is a promise of God's welcome home to us. It should be incredibly warm and forgiving but not always felt that way.

CALLING GOD *FATHER*

I remember the first time I saw Jane (not her real name). She crept into the room and slid tentatively into a chair. Everything about her shouted pain, and the story she came to tell confirmed it. In the weeks that followed she acted on her intention that first day—she came home to God in a final desperate attempt to find peace and healing in her life. It was only the beginning of a long process of change for her.

One measure of her hurt was that Jane could not address God as Father. She had had no experience of being lovingly fathered, and most of the other male figures in her life had been abusive. The *father* word carried a load of pain for her, as did *home*—both words packed with unfulfilled expectation.

This is true for many who come home to God, both men and women. Fortunately, not all have had a father physically abuse them, but the pain is almost as great if a parent turns a blind eye to someone else harming them. Others sense an empty void because their father (or mother) was unapproachable and distant. It leaves a scar when the child realizes what might have been. Lack of personal safety in childhood is felt acutely and deeply and is so damaging that grief over abandonment can persist for years in adulthood, even lifelong. Being seen and loved by our parents, we feel is our birthright.

I saw this again in the story of a man I met recently. He showed me his Ancestry app results after he had provided a DNA sample to the site. He signed up because he had a very specific and nagging hunger to know more about where he came from. His mother had told him only when he reached his early twenties that the man he had grown up believing was his birth father was not so. Shocked and hurting, especially by the deceit, he pressed her for more details, but she knew only the name of the man whose genes he carried, and no further details about him.

At the time of this disclosure, the man was enthusiastically getting on with adult life and so let the issue lie. But now married and with children of his own, he wanted to know more about what he had inherited, and how he fitted into the community around him. Interestingly, his ancestry search uncovered a whole network of relatives, most of whom allowed contact. Some even lived nearby. He appreciated these new connections, but still he had not found his biological father. The continuing hunger emphasized how important it was for him (and for us too) to know where we belong, where we are accepted, where we can call home.

The danger is that when our lived experience falls short of normal human expectations and gives us less than God's plan for human thriving, it can take time for us to enter into all that is on offer when we come home to God. The hurts and scars become even more distressing when we get glimpses of God's good intentions for the people he has made.

GOD OUR PARENT

In the years that I knew her, Jane showed growing maturity and godly character. Coming home to God opened new dimensions of life for her, and she began reaching out to others who had experienced trauma at home as she had. She would speak of Jesus, pray to him, delight in reading his actions and words in the Gospels. She recognized in him someone who had known shame even greater than she had, and who loved her and welcomed her into a safe place. She started to learn to trust him as a brother. But after many years of healing, she still could not call God *Father*.

Some people consider *father* too narrow a name for God, arguing that what the Scriptures teach is that God is our *parent*, not a gender description. They remind us that at times God is also described as acting towards us like a mother. Nevertheless, we have in Scripture the example of Jesus calling God *Father*, and we see in the Gospels both how revealing this is and how unexpected. It speaks of intimacy and trust, not just obedience, though a first-century Palestinian father would of course have expected obedience from his children. The understanding of the great high God as a caring father is found in the Old Testament, but it is only as we hear Jesus use the title of *Son* for himself that the word *Father* takes on the full resonance of access and intimacy.

Jesus displays this intimacy when he models prayer to his followers. He tells them to begin with the words "Our Father" too, a precious reminder when we pray that we inherit the gift of calling him *Father* and all the benefits that go with that expectation.

THE *GOOD* FATHER

Sometime later in her journey to recovery, I suggested to Jane that while she was still hesitating to address God as *Father* because of its painful family associations, she could put *good* with it—and so call God the *Good Father*. The pattern for this comes from Jesus' own teaching. On one occasion he described himself to his disciples as a shepherd. They knew that not all shepherds were trustworthy—some neglected their sheep, even abandoning them in the face of danger. In fact, Jesus specifically mentions bad shepherds in contrast to himself in John 10. Nevertheless, he adopts the word, calling himself the *Good Shepherd*. His hearers knew what made a poor shepherd, but they also knew what was expected of a good shepherd. That was the kind of care they experienced from Jesus; he was indeed the *good shepherd*.

The Good Shepherd was one of the first representations of the Christian faith. Drawings of Jesus as a shepherd are found, for example, in Rome's second-century catacombs. That is earlier than when the most recognized Christian symbol, the cross, was popularized by Emperor Constantine two centuries later.

What is important, however, is that even if our lived experience of our own father falls short of the ideal, we can rejoice in having in God a *Good Father*, whatever our history. I described in a previous book that although my human father did not disappoint me, life events and family demands caused me to take on adult responsibilities too early in my teenage years. As a consequence, I long felt I had not been parented adequately. God's gift to me in a little chapel in California where I was studying was an experience of the warmth of calling God *Father*. Each morning in that chapel as we prayed the "Our Father," the early morning rays of the sun reached me through a window and gave me their *Father* warmth and promised healing.[2]

JANE'S HEALING BEGINS

For Jane, it was a more gradual learning to call God the *Good Father*. The years after coming home to God were up and down for her. The issues to be dealt with were immense as God began healing the wounds from her past. But in her appearance, in relating to her sons, in her other relationships, she discovered new ways to live because of God's grace in her. The *Good Father* had welcomed her home with loving arms, and that made all the difference.

That is what our Welsh professor needed to experience. He saw through his childhood eyes a faith that swallowed up its adherents, and he feared losing autonomy in acknowledging an all-powerful Creator. Yet he longed for intimacy with the God of his mother. In response to his questioning, I had made a preposterous claim! The God of the universe welcomes a personal relationship with each of us. I still affirm that with fear and trembling, for it is the heart of the gospel, our Christian good news. We *can* have a close relationship with God. He is the *Good Father*. Loving relationship, not abuse nor neglect, are the very nature of this God. It is no wonder that we who are created in God's image (Gen 1:26) long for love and intimacy too. This is the great news Jesus unveils in his story of the father welcoming the prodigal son home.

HOW CAN WE DESCRIBE LOVE LIKE THIS?

When the prodigal appeared on the horizon, Jesus' story says that the father did more than allow him back into the house as his son, however

2. Turner, *Finding Your Voice*, 126.

unexpected and welcoming that was. His open arms spoke emphatically of loving and forgiving his son and restoring him to the relationship a father always hopes for in a son. Love given and love returned.

How can we describe this deep forgiving love today in our own lives? We know that it is much more than breathy songs on Valentine's Day dominating the media. Many of us have experienced the spark, the chemistry, with another that we hope is the longed-for attachment to carry us into a lasting relationship. But even that—the chemistry of attraction—does not get to the essence of love. Real love is harder to grasp. It includes seeing and accepting the person for just who they are but also longing for much more for and from them. It can persist in that expectation through better and worse, richer and poorer, in sickness and in health. Most importantly, it is warmth that can be felt in our heart, more than it is known in our head or even in our body. We recognize it when we see it in real life, specifically when we see it in action, because love shows itself in action.

Perhaps that is why the apostle Paul's description of love, words often recited at weddings, need to be listened to carefully. He expresses love way beyond an infatuation or an expectation of what each party can get out of a relationship. He places love firmly in acts of selfless giving.

> Love is patient, love is kind. It does not envy, it does not boast, it is not proud. It does not dishonor others, it is not self-seeking, it is not easily angered, it keeps no record of wrongs. Love does not delight in evil but rejoices with the truth. It always protects, always trusts, always hopes, always perseveres. (1 Cor 13:4–7)

God's love is like this. It is acting, always giving, and we are created to receive this kind of love. No wonder we long for it. And when we have experienced it personally, we are much better equipped to pass it on in our other relationships, including in our marriage.

WE STRUGGLE TO LOVE

Recently a grandson was telling me his school friends were regularly placing internet bets on sporting events. When dismay showed on my face at how easily these teenagers were getting into gambling, he quickly added, "They say there is nothing wrong with using a bit of your own money to have fun. It's just a form of entertainment." My first instinct was to warn him about the dangers of addiction, to tell him of people I knew whose lives and families were torn apart by gambling losses.

Instead, I talked about a deeper problem—people not caring for anyone other than themselves. Getting rich through gambling is only possible by taking advantage of another person's loss. How can you be loving a person while you are fleecing them, even if you do not know who they are? Moreover, victims are often people who can ill afford the loss of anything but in desperation are risking further harm in the hope of getting themselves out of an overwhelming financial bind.

I think my grandson heard me. But the conversation reminded me how difficult it is to love, to be generous, and how hard it is to swim against a culture's selfish way of living with only our own resources. Self-giving love for others does not come easily. That is why the apostle John says we love best when we have received God's love, when we experience his generosity towards us personally. God is the very essence of love, John declares. His divine love is the first love; ours, the second. It flows out of the love we have received (1 John 4:16, 19).

UNDESERVED LOVE

Do we deserve God's love? The prodigal son did not deserve to be accepted back into the family, and he knew it. A glib written apology about how selfish he had been, asking for his inheritance and leaving the family toil to his father and brother, would not have gotten him through the door. But when the sheer desperation of hunger and loss drove him to get up and head for home, it was his father's kindness and mercy, a desire to once again enjoy a relationship with his son, that welcomed him in.

God's offer of deep relationship with us is the same. God has no obligation to take us back, even though he created us and wants to enjoy intimacy with us. It is the sheer generosity of this Good Father that greets us when we turn for home.

Moreover, God's acceptance of us, so unconditional when we experience it, does not settle for leaving us where we are. Just as we might imagine the prodigal's father has hopes for new attitudes and habits developing in his younger son, so the God welcoming us into a new intimacy offers us the prospect of growing maturity and deep spirituality. How God the Holy Spirit goes about doing this we will explore in later chapters.

THE COST OF GOD'S GENEROSITY

There is a cost to be paid, however, to rescue wayward humans who have strayed from home. And because the Good Father mourns the breaking of his relationship with us, he does something about it. God's act of love and generosity begins with Jesus laying aside his divine privileges and coming into human life to identify with us. It leads to his sacrificial death on a gruesome cross (Phil 2:6–8).

The cross is not God being angry. As Richard Foster says, "Nothing could be further from the truth. Love, not anger brought Jesus to the cross. Golgotha came as a result of God's great desire to forgive, not his reluctance."[3] But God is holy, separated from us because of our sin, and there is great mystery in uniting this with his love.

Some claim the Old Testament always emphasizes that God is holy, untouchable, distant, while the God of the New Testament shows us a face of love. But God is eternally constant—both forever holy and forever loving.

A holy God does not push us away—most of all he wants a relationship with us. We get a little retrospective glimpse of this desire for companionship in Gen 3:8. The Creator's daily practice was to walk with the people he had made in the cool of the day in the beautiful garden he had gifted to them. But when they defied the boundaries set for them, it shattered the relationship. We are told that in their shame they hid *from* rather than walked *with* God.

It was the Creator's loss too. Right there in the garden God promised that one day someone would come to put things right and open the way to a generous restoration of intimacy.

That God values connection with us, even created humans for that purpose, is a startling thought. It surely counters any suggestion that desiring relationship is a sign of weakness or that in seeking us out, God's perfection, sovereignty, and omnipotence are threatened. Indeed, loving relationships are the heart of the Godhead, the Scriptures teach us, and later we will explore this further. For now, it is important to affirm we humans were made for this kind of intimacy, indeed hunger for it, because relating deeply is Godlike, like the oneness of Father, Son, and Spirit—in whose image we were made.

3. Foster, *Celebration of Discipline*, 143.

ONLY A HOLY GOD

But what of this other characteristic of God—that he is holy? J. I. Packer says that the word *holy* "focuses attention on everything that in God makes him a proper object of awe and worship and reverent fear, and that serves to remind his human creatures how ungodlike they really are."[4] Yes, we know this God, this divine Creator, is far above us, and we should worship him in awe and gratitude for his magnificent universe; we should wonder at the complexity and fine-tuning of the people he has made; and we should not presume on his kindness nor approach him unworthily. Pulitzer Prize–winner Annie Dillard questions those who treat God too carelessly, saying, "Does anyone have the foggiest idea of what sort of power we so blithely invoke? . . . We should all be wearing crash helmets."[5]

But *holy* is not just a word about power. In the church I attended as a child, the words from Ps 96:9 (in King James English) were written large in an archway over the front wall of the sanctuary: *Worship the Lord in the beauty of holiness*. I puzzled over its meaning many a Sunday. I knew at least it was not referring to my holiness, which was sadly lacking, so how was God's holiness beautiful, not scary in the way power is? I felt, despite the supposed beauty, that God's holiness spoke of a fearsome separation from a God whose holiness I could not match.

As an adult now and having experienced more of this broken world, I know how desperately we want justice, for things to be put right. We do want a powerful God, but our human experience is that power can be dangerous, that power often corrupts and drives out love. The tyrants, the autocrats, the superrich of this world easily lose any vestige of empathy, let alone love. They even exploit their own followers, having an eye only for their own interests. So how can God be both powerful and loving? Is he safe, this all-powerful God?

I am confident, however, that as we respond to God the Good Father and worship him in awe and wonder at his unfailing love, it is his holiness that reassures us that he will not exploit or enslave us, that he cannot do wrong. God's holiness is our guarantee that he is safe. We can open ourselves to an incredible intimacy with a loving *and* holy God because he wants only the best for us. We can call him Good Father, and know he is safe as well as powerful because he is holy. Holiness, as the psalm said, is indeed beautiful.

4. Packer, *Knowing God*, 5.

5. Quoted in Peterson, *Contemplative Pastor*, 90.

JESUS IS RELATIONSHIP SAFETY

Jesus displayed this relationship safety as he traveled Palestine in his years of earthly ministry. He called to follow him an unlikely bunch of people who did not understand his mission very well at first but still responded to his discipleship call, sensing something godly and unique in this man. They grew in their trust of him as they slowly comprehended what it meant to be his disciple. Among them was a hated money man, a few hardy and rough fishermen, a former zealot radical, a skeptical Thomas—yet all learned from their Master what safe relationships looked like. They also saw in his example the incredible intimacy possible with a holy God.

Jesus' interactions with women also showed a safe, reassuring love. On one occasion critics brought to him someone they said was caught in the act of adultery (though they did not similarly shame the man involved with her). They expected Jesus to condemn her or perhaps refuse to have anything to do with her, fearing contamination. Instead, he treated her kindly when she was paraded before him (John 8:2–11).

Another time, hard-pressed by people crowding around him, Jesus felt power go out of him and stopped for a woman who reached out through the throng hoping that just a touch of his robe would heal her of the bleeding that had ostracized her twelve years. The woman was healed and fell at his feet, shamed and trembling with fear. When she had told her story, Jesus gently called her daughter, commending her faith and freeing her of her social disgrace. She went away acknowledged, healed, and rejoicing (Mark 5:24b–34).

A SHOWER OF SAFE GRACE

Paul Gioia wrote a haunting song based on this incident. The refrain always moves me by its picture of God's reliable and safe grace.

> There's nothing I can do
> To scare your grace away
> No foolish thing I do
> No foolish thing I say
> Under the shadow of a cross
> Under a shower of grace
> I feel the Father's healing hands
> And touch his smiling face.[6]

6. Gioia, "Shower of Grace," based on Mark 5:21–34 (in Gioia, *Shower*, 11).

God the Holy Spirit is safe too, and I remember a friend discovering that. She had been expressing her fear that a controlling God could come upon her, override her will, and force her to fall down under the influence of the Spirit. She knew what it was like to feel small and frightened in the presence of abusive human power, but she found Jesus' parting promise to his disciples was to be the gift of the Spirit *in his place* (John 15:26, 16:7). This Jesus she trusted from the Gospel stories was gentle, understanding, considerate of people. If this Spirit, she realized, was to be Jesus' presence with them, no more, no less, then she could trust this Spirit. He would be holy, safe. In his humanity and holiness Jesus shows us the character of the God who invites us into safe intimacy.

Most significant of all, however, this God who invites us to approach him, to call him Father, is the one who *in Jesus* gave himself for us in human flesh on the Roman cross—at considerable cost, well beyond the physical pain. When we hear Jesus cry from the cross, "My God, my God, why have you forsaken me?" (Matt 27:46) we realize his biggest cost was experiencing a severed connection to God his Father. That is our biggest loss too. But because Jesus took our disordered and damaged place, we do not need to continue in that condition any longer. With Jesus' cry, "It is finished!" (John 19:30) we are assured the way is now open to a safe, loving relationship with the Father.

WHAT HAPPENS NEXT?

In Jesus' story, turning for home is the prodigal's repentance, however self-serving it may appear. It opens a new chapter of his life. Would he have welcomed all the new possibilities now open to him or lapsed back into taking them for granted? Would he have daily appreciated relating again to his father? The same open arms and forgiveness that the prodigal saw as he approached home are ours as well when we come home to the Good Father.

However, we often do not appreciate the full privilege and comfort of this incredible intimacy when we first come in from the cold. We enter confidently knowing we are wanted and accepted as we respond to God's unfailing love, but we may be tempted to think that is all we need. But we must remember *who* it is that calls us home. God has great plans for his returning children. Not only is this invitation an incredible privilege, it is only the beginning of what can be a life-changing relationship, better than life itself. There is so much more on offer in the Father's house.

But there is something that the Father must attend to first. We were probably damaged by our time away from home and in need of recovery. Healing our hurts and scars and overcoming any past trauma must be treated. That is the subject of the next chapter as we explore what is available to us now at home with the Good Father.

RESPONDING

- If calling God *Father* has been difficult for you, can you acknowledge him as your *Good* Father? Let that begin your appreciation of how much he loves you.
- Knowing you can be forgiven is perhaps an issue for you. But because of Jesus, there now need be no condemnation (Rom 8:1–2). There is nothing you can do to drive his grace away. Ponder again the words of Paul Gioia's song. Are you able to welcome this *shower of grace* today, even if you have been wary of it before?
- Only a holy God is safe. Focus on *who* is inviting you into this incredible intimacy and reach out to touch his smiling face.

3

Hurts and Scars

It is a lie—any talk of God
that does not
comfort you.

—Meister Eckhart, medieval German theologian and mystic (1260–1327)

Some years ago, I tried to cultivate zucchini plants in the sandy soil of our first Perth garden. Despite being a successful zucchini grower previously in the east of Australia, here in Perth I was unable to make my zucchinis set fruit in the poverty of the sand dune on which we lived. I invested in liquid fertilizer and carefully watered it in, almost daily. Now my zucchini plants had no excuse. They had plenty of nutrients to assist their growth, readily available all around them in the soil. But still, they did not grow!

It seemed to me they were muttering every time I checked on them: "She's wasting a lot of money buying this fertilizer. Her family doesn't even like zucchini! We will just not take up the nutrients even though she has spread it all around us." That attitude (if zucchini plants were indeed capable of it) did not help either them or me. Their refusal to take what I offered them was actually more disappointing than their poor growth. Sometimes we are like that with what God offers to us, now we are home. God's *more* is there for the asking, for us to take. Maturity, flourishing are on offer—all that the Father longs to see in us. And it is in our best interests to take it!

Rather than think of ourselves as zucchini plants (perhaps you do not like zucchini either), we are urged in the Scriptures to think of ourselves as sons and daughters of a loving Father. We have come home and entered the family home with all that it offers. We have been embraced and enfolded into a wonderful relationship with the Creator of the universe. Are we expecting enough? Are we satisfied with our lives? Are we growing spiritually, thriving? There is so much more which could be ours if we take it. We cannot generate that growth ourselves, but we can make sure we are thriving in the light and fertilizer of God's love.

FAILING TO THRIVE

The word *thrive* has long had a special resonance for me, or rather, *failure to thrive* has! Soon after he was born, our second son was given this heavy diagnosis. Something was wrong! Cystic fibrosis was mentioned. Or not getting enough milk? Or some kind of obstruction? For a few months, we shared the experience of other parents whose dreams for their new baby are inexplicably clouded. However, one day at about three months old, our son was on the pediatrician's examining table as the doctor tried again to find a reason for his continuing low weight and skinny frame. Suddenly, he pushed himself up from his tummy on his hands and looked directly into the face of the doctor. It was clear he had no developmental delay! In fact, later he sat up early and walked at nine months. The label *failure to thrive* disappeared, but he was discovered to have a congenital throat constriction which he was gradually freed of as his body grew!

Some who have come home and experienced God's saving grace could be diagnosed as failing to thrive. To encourage you to thrive, here are some suggestions. The first is to simply luxuriate in the Good Father's love as he begins his healing work in you.

WHAT HAPPENS NEXT FOR RETURNING PRODIGALS

Jesus continued his story of the father celebrating the homecoming of his prodigal son with these words to his servants:

> Quick! Bring the best robe and put it on him. Put a ring on his finger and sandals on his feet. Bring the fattened calf and kill it. Let's have a feast and celebrate. For this son of mine was dead and is alive again; he was lost and is found. (Luke 15:22–24)

The homecoming to the loving father's house was just the beginning for the prodigal. He presumably would need a good wash before putting on fresh clothes to enjoy the promised welcome home party. After that, a long sleep and some regular meals would be on the agenda. Perhaps he had actual scars from sleeping rough and lack of food. He may need time to heal physically, but he would especially need emotional healing. Hopefully, reconciliation with his estranged brother was possible and he would put in some hard farm work to begin restoration of what he had skimmed off the family.

Being loved and accepted by his father made physical and emotional healing possible, but it would not have been automatic. He would have to commit himself to the recovery process. In addition to the healing of emotional hurts and scars from his previous errant life, entering again into the privileges of being a son would involve behavior change too. Bad habits and attitudes he had acquired would become obvious and need correction. He could even need sharp reminders of conduct appropriate for a son who should again be contributing to the family.

Jesus' father-with-two-sons story does not have this next episode, but we can imagine it and let it challenge us to ask what is next for us after we have responded to the Good Father's generous welcome home. Do we just kick off our shoes and relax into our new freedom? It would be tragic if we were satisfied merely to settle down inside the family walls and thank our lucky stars we were let in. Even more tragic if we just crept in the door, hardly daring to think we have access to anything by right, and retreat to the attic ashamed to look anyone in the face. Yes, we come home with all the scars of our misadventures; we have learned the hard way not to trust people or ourselves. We may even have gotten into the habit of setting our sights unnecessarily low. But Jesus' prodigal son story will not settle for that. Whether we have wandered far like a prodigal, or stayed at home internalizing our rebellion, there are continuing consequences of past damaging practices and wrong choices which will call for recovery and perhaps restitution.

The prodigal's father celebrates his son's homecoming, and Jesus intends that we, too, enjoy and use to the full the privileges and responsibilities of being God's returned children—men and women who are freed, accepted, forgiven, and loved. We are promised all the resources of a Father who created and directs the riches of this world. How do we tap into these? What difference does it make that we now live in the Good Father's house? This is what this book is about as we further explore what it means to be sons and daughters of a generous and Good Father.

WE ARE A NEW CREATION

In one sense, when we come home to God, we are already a new creation. As the apostle Paul told the Corinthian Christians (who were no model of perfection), "The old life is gone; a new life emerges!" (2 Cor 5:17 MSG). The priority for change for us, of course, is the healing of relationships, but we also need the Spirit's help to deal with destructive habits and ways of thinking as the re-Creator sets about developing the character expected of us. Sometimes this may surprise us with immediate reformation, but more often growth and maturity come through unexpected trials and hard work; however, we can anticipate a lifetime of adjusting to the privileges now ours as restored sons and daughters of the Good Father.

RECOVERY FROM SHAME

While he sat among the pigs, the prodigal imagined that the best he could expect back home was to slip into the old house and forego his "son" status, but at least he would have a roof over his head and something in his stomach. What his father offered was so much more: hugs and kisses, a welcome home party, and restoration to the family, despite the dishonor he had caused them—sure signs he was accepted back.

We know from experience that acceptance and forgiveness are great gifts—just as essential as food and shelter. We long for them, but crucially, we hunger even more to be free of shame. Whether it is shame arising from what we have done or shame from what others have done to us, shame hangs on us like a bad smell and disturbs our mind and heart as well as our nose! But the good news is that recovery from shame is on offer when God welcomes us with grace-filled arms. We can base the rest of our lives on this display of grace.

A glimpse of this possibility comes through four Bible characters surprisingly mentioned in the first chapter of Matthew's Gospel. In longing for an all-conquering Messiah, Matthew's Hebrew readers would have expected any description of Jesus' lineage to be anchored in their covenant history with a genealogy. So Matthew starts with one going back to their founding father, Abraham. Traditionally such a Hebrew list of the time would give the male names of fathers and their sons down through the generations, but in four cases Matthew mentions the mother too. For each of these women there is a story of unexpected redemption, a story of grace overcoming shame.

The first mentioned is Tamar. Denied her traditional right to bear children in the family of her husband after his death, she took things into her own hands. She seduced her father-in-law, Judah, by pretending to be a prostitute and became pregnant by him (Gen 38). We are not told if Tamar was later accepted by his family, but Judah's guilt was certainly exposed by the pregnancy. Nevertheless, the one considered the older of the resulting twins, grandson to the patriarch Jacob, was recognized in the line to Jesus, and Tamar as his mother.

The second name is Rahab, known in several places in the Bible as "the prostitute."[1] Rahab plied her trade in a house on the wall of Jericho, the fortified city the Hebrews needed to capture to cross the Jordan and take the land God had promised them. When Israelite men slipped into her house to spy out the city and assess the mood of the people, pagan Rahab voiced her belief that their God was powerful and would deliver them the victory. She demonstrated her faith by hiding the spies and helping them escape, asking only for her family to be saved in the coming battle. She was indeed rescued and later accepted by the Hebrews, "marrying in" to become part of the line to Jesus.

The final two women were more acted upon than acting, victims of a power differential. Ruth was a refugee from the country of Moab whose people were forbidden to mix with the Israelites. But her loyalty to the Hebrews' God and her mother-in-law resulted in her being rescued from poverty and exclusion through marriage, becoming great-grandmother to King David.

Several generations later, Bathsheba (her name is not given in Matthew's list) was a victim of that king's power. David took the beautiful young woman and had her husband killed to distract from his rape. She lost the baby resulting from the assault but later was honored as queen to David and mother to another son, Solomon.

WHAT DOES GOD DO ABOUT OUR PAST?

I sometimes wonder how each of these women would have felt unexpectedly finding themselves in the line to the Messiah. It might have been not only comforting but empowering. The culture of the time generally gave

1. Heb 11:31, Jas 2:25, and in the story of Josh 2:1, 6:22–23.

women little personal agency, subjecting them to generational and gender limitations as well as abuse. Mostly, it was family that provided the acceptance and security they needed, though often their marriage was shadowed by the circumstances of its creation. Nevertheless, their exceptional inclusion in the royal line to Jesus encourages us that coming home to God offers redemption from our past, no matter our culture or our personal mistreatment.

I wish I had shown Jane (whose story I tell in the previous chapter) the power of these stories. We certainly talked about Jesus' grace-filled interactions with women. In these, Jesus defied his culture by demonstrating a particularly warm heart towards those most excluded in his day. This is very clear in the many interactions he had with people recounted in the Gospels. In addition to the woman caught committing adultery that he saved from stoning, there was a hated tax collector up a tree whom Jesus acknowledged and dined with, and whose life he turned around. And the woman ritually and practically ostracized by years of bleeding, who came tentatively and secretly through the crowds to touch Jesus for healing. His power to heal not only physical scars but emotional hurt was clearly demonstrated in his earthly ministry and reminds us that moving beyond shame is still available to all.

We also see Jesus offer a similar loving acknowledgement and healing to his disciple Peter. Good old Peter. Always the first to respond to a challenge, the first with a declaration of loyalty, the first with a sword. Then, under pressure, he denies knowing Jesus, not once but three times. Sometimes I think Peter gets a bad rap. At least he is *in* the courtyard of the high priest the night Jesus was arrested, as close as possible to him, when most of the other disciples are scattered to the four winds in fear. The same applies to Simon Peter's attempt to walk on water to get to his Master. Even if after one or two steps his faith falters and he falls, he was willing to give it a go.

Nevertheless, his failures were often as large as his courage, and after the courtyard denials he remembered Jesus' words and realized with shame what he had done, going outside and weeping "bitterly" (Matt 26:75). How comforting it must have been for him that Jesus, in the days after his resurrection, singled Peter out for restoration when in despair and bewilderment he has gone back up north to return to his fishing (John 21:15–19). Matching his denials, Jesus recommissions him three times. How good to be wanted by the Master despite your very evident failure! How empowering for his later leadership to be reassured of Jesus' acceptance and forgiveness.

GENERATIONAL HARM

Today we increasingly recognize the damage done in early years to those whose trust has been violated through abuse or neglect. We also know that the path to recovery of personhood and godly functional behavior takes time. In many ways, all of us have been damaged by sin—that of others and of our own.

Parents, for example, no matter how faithful, can carry and pass on generational pain to their offspring, with dysfunctional patterns observed over multiple generations. The importance of this is now recognized in explaining problems in families and in groups through forms of chronic anxiety and the vulnerabilities of leaders (and parents).[2]

There are some fascinating and tragic patterns of generational harm passed down generations in Old Testament stories. One example is that of Abraham's family. The admired patriarch resorted to deceit when he felt threatened by Pharaoh because of Sarah's beauty, and passed her off as his sister, not his wife. Later he used that tactic a second time, and his son Isaac also stooped to the same deceit. But most memorably, Abraham's grandson Jacob, whose name became synonymous with "cunning swindler," robbed his brother of his rightful blessing through deceiving his father.

There is healing through Jesus for this kind of hurt and scar. In the time of the Hebrew prophet Jeremiah, they had a saying: "The parents have eaten sour grapes, and the children's teeth are set on edge" (Jer 31:29). The prophet references this adage in offering God-hope that in years to come, through the new relationships the promised Messiah would bring, things will be different. No need, he said, for the children of deficient parents to taste sour grapes! Inherited generational pain will be replaced because each person will have the opportunity to receive God's grace and healing.

We are also aware that the school playground, and the even rougher playground of adult relationships, have damaged many of us. Catastrophic life events can damage us too. In fact, the very survival patterns we develop to endure a cruel world may in the long run lead us into harmful ways of living. When we have been let down badly, we need to learn to trust again; and where we have acquired attitudes to ourselves or others that are destructive or exploitative, we must grow new ones.

2. Cuss in *The Expectation Gap* recommends use of the genogram to understand our own or another's responses.

THE HEALING BEGINS

The Good Father begins the process of healing as soon as we come home, but it is not forced on us. We can either say yes or ignore the offer. Maybe our behavior needs to change. The Holy Spirit may lovingly draw attention to a particular conduct or attitude that must be modified or abandoned, and we feel a special urgency grow in our awareness, so it becomes a growth issue. Perhaps the healing is to take the sting out of painful memories or to teach us how to react differently in specific situations as we begin to think of ourselves differently through the prism of God's love and acceptance.

These convictions and the consequent recovery may come through people, from biblical wisdom, or from insights gained by reflecting on the events in our lives. There are many possible avenues available to God's transforming Spirit. With our cooperation, the re-creating God begins our transformation into people fully at home with the Good Father.

However, in a very real sense, we are always like the alcoholics who find help through Alcoholics Anonymous. We are *recovering*, not *recovered*. We never graduate from this process and continue to need the ongoing support and care of the "higher power" whom we are getting to know personally as our Good Father.

This applies in many arenas. After writing a recent very revealing autobiography telling the story of her psychological condition, trichotillomania, Adele Dumont was pressed by the interviewer in a podcast[3] to say if she expected to ever be finally free of the compulsion to pull out her hair. She, too, referenced the *recovering*, not *recovered* insight from AA.[4]

HEALING THE WOUNDS OF TRAUMA

This chapter is called the more general "Hurts and Scars" because for some of us, the deeply damaging childhood abuse that Jane suffered is not our experience. Nor has something in adulthood derailed us so greatly. Nevertheless, all of us are damaged and less than the Creator intended. By coming home, God gives us the possibility of growing towards the person we were created to be. New learnings in how to live become available, treating others selflessly and kindly seems possible, as we grow into becoming more like Jesus to the end of our days.

3. Australian Broadcasting Corporation's *Conversations*.
4. Dumont, *Pulling*.

But for some, *hurts* and *scars* are not strong enough words. These people have been damaged by *trauma*, affecting their whole thinking, feeling, being, and life circumstances. Trauma becomes part of their self-identity, how they understand their *self*. We now speak of trauma-informed practice and trauma-informed counseling, acknowledging the greater degree of harm that some people experience. Yet even out of trauma I have seen God's grace bring healing, as he did for Jane.

While teaching in Africa I discovered a local program that addressed the consequences of trauma.[5] Designed to be conducted over a weekend or through a series of weekly sessions, the first time I used it we only had a few sessions available within a week's conference full of other courses and activities.

The pastors and leaders present came from countries where the churches discourage expressing grief or discussing trauma, yet many of these women had suffered the loss of husband, children, homes, or livelihoods. Some had been victims of rape used as a tool of war or experienced domestic violence; some were second or third wives whose children and financial needs were neglected. Anticipating that even mentioning trauma would be disturbing, we made provision for counseling to be offered alongside the teaching sessions, and I invited a close friend, a psychologist, to be co-facilitator. Although in the past I have seen great value in peer group sharing, the conference format meant we had to forego using even simple groups. Instead, we included in each session times of sharing with a "prayer partner." We urged the fifty women to sit and pair every session with a woman who spoke their mother tongue, knowing that heart language is important for deep sharing. It became obvious as the week went on that this opened a very significant door of healing for them that lasted well beyond the conference.

We facilitators began with telling a little of our own story. My colleague described a physical limitation that the local women could relate to. In her early nursing career, she had been blinded in one eye by an exploding hypodermic needle. It has affected her movements ever since, leading to a fear of falling. The immediate impact and the subsequent operations created genuine and ongoing trauma.

In contrast, I was reluctant to think of my story as trauma—though it included multiple miscarriages happening in foreign countries.[6] It seemed

5. See Hill et al., *Healing the Wounds of Trauma*.

6. See Turner, *Finding Your Voice*, 2.

a long time in the past, and later I gave birth to three healthy babies. Nevertheless, whatever our life experiences, we all need to address the very real and central question of suffering. When bad things happen to us, can we still trust God? Is he really loving? And can our heart wounds really be healed? That was our starting point.

The women began stutteringly and only at intervals to name their pain to their prayer partners. But the conversations did begin, and the relief from permission to talk about their heart wounds was palpable. We heard the next day that sharing-pair conversations started in the sessions were continuing into the night within their shared accommodation, as the women found companionship and empathy on their journey of healing.

On the final day we retold the story of Jesus' death on the cross, a story these women knew well but, like many of us, thought applied only to Jesus bearing our sin of disobeying and resisting our Creator. Instead, we encouraged them to take their pain to the cross and write down confidentially what they wanted to bring to Jesus. Then we invited them to solemnly and prayerfully pin their Post-it notes to a rough cross we had put together. As a symbol of the emotional healing available in the crucified and risen Savior, these records of their pain were destroyed.

Restoration begins when we come home to the Good Father, and sometimes the Spirit brings instant relief and recovery, taking the sting out of memories or giving us unexpected and unearned love and forgiveness for a perpetrator. More often, healing, and especially forgiving, is a gradual process encouraged by small gains that may continue to the day we are united with Jesus in glory.

WHAT IF YOU DO NOT DIE TONIGHT?

Sometimes the question is asked, "What if you were to die tonight? Are you ready to meet your Creator?" But there is another question: "What if you do not die tonight? How are you to go on living, thriving?" Our quality of life should be different now we have come home. Jesus said he came to bring a new, full life (John 10:10). In the house of the Father, we are heirs through him of everything the Creator of this world offers. We are heirs with access here, as well as in the life to come. So how do we enter into these riches?

The answer, of course, cannot be a specified program: Step 1, then Step 2, then Step 3, and you will have it made! We know that human life for the most part does not work like that, however many good-life gurus try to sell us their fail-safe system. A thriving, flourishing life is about relationships—with God, with ourself, and with others. Human relationships cannot be so easily programmed. By the time we come home, we will have had years of thinking too little of God, too little (or too much) of ourselves, and too little of others. But we can know that within this new Good Father relationship, we will have reason to revise upwards our expectation of what is possible because we trust God's word and his promises.

There are many ways to describe how we are changed and receive these new qualities of life after coming home. Each of these is a gift freely given to us by the Giver of all good gifts. Each is an experience of grace, just like the Father's amazing grace that first welcomed us in. But as in the choice to come home, each requires our consent and our cooperation at every phase. We are never imposed on by God. We are always invited to *ask* for this "more" because there is no way we can earn it. But we must *ask*.

There are possibilities of healing, character growth, power—all available from the hand of the One who comes out to meet us and who wants most of all to restore the family relationships. Such possible transformations are mentioned here but briefly, so we can begin to anticipate the full riches available to us, now we have come home. In later chapters of this book, we will explore additional dimensions of this wonderful relationship with the Good Father which we have begun. But the starting point is how we are now thinking of ourselves.

CALL OURSELVES SAINTS?

One writer,[7] focusing on the transformation that the Spirit brings to those who choose to follow Jesus, brings together two of Paul's statements about our condition: "There is no condemnation for those who are in Christ Jesus," and, "If anyone is in Christ, the new creation has come: The old has gone, the new is here!" (Rom 8:1 and 2 Cor 5:17) The writer urges Christians to think of themselves not as *sinners* but as *saints*. True, even "in Christ Jesus" we fall short of what God expects of us and continue to sin, but our status has now changed. Some people recognize this by calling themselves "sinners saved by grace," but the usual word New Testament writers use for Christians is *saints*. That can be startling to hear applied to ourselves, but let us use it! It is a wonderful reminder of our change of status.

7. Smith, *Good and Beautiful God.*

At a recent funeral, the officiating minister searched widely to find a word to describe the friend and mentor whom we had assembled to remember on his death. He settled on calling our friend a *saint*. This man's life had touched so many. Even a casual conversation with him left you feeling heard and blessed, challenged, and wiser in the ways of God. It was a fitting word for our friend. But for me, for you, for all who have come home to the Good Father, can we think of ourself as a *saint*? Yes![8]

It is a matter of emphasis. When we are challenged to live God's way, considering ourselves made clean and pure by God, calling ourselves *saints* reminds us to draw on the resources at our disposal through the Holy Spirit and to behave and love and serve as the new person we are. Conversely, calling ourselves *sinners* might build in an expectation, or even an excuse, that inevitably we will fail God's standards. That puts the focus back on ourself and our weaknesses.

Even better, knowing ourselves as God's family and heirs points to all that is available now we are home and with our brothers and sisters. We know we have the possibility to live differently and fully with the Holy Spirit's power, luxuriating in being sons and daughters of a welcoming Father. That we will explore later.

But first, we must see that Jesus urges us to confidently ask our generous God for what we need to live as he intended when we were created. That is our next chapter.

RESPONDING

- Where do you live in the Good Father's house—in the royal suite or the servants' quarters? Or are you hiding in the attic, still wracked by shame?
- Which sign would you choose to display on your life right now: "Please be patient. I'm under construction" or "Under new management"? Or do you dare to say "Saint" as the apostle Paul uses it in 1 Corinthians 1:2 (KJV)?

8. If you are still worried about calling yourself a saint, take a cue from Mandy Smith whose book, *Confessions of an Amateur Saint*, pairs the term *amateur* with *saint* in its original sense of choosing to immerse oneself in something for the love of it.

- What do you picture *thriving* looks like in your life? Move towards it with the Holy Spirit's wisdom and help. Claim the promises of Psalm 92:12–15.

4

Simply Ask

Don't bargain with God. Be direct. Ask for what you need. This isn't a cat-and-mouse, hide-and-seek game we're in. If your child asks for bread, do you trick him with sawdust? If he asks for fish, do you scare him with a live snake on his plate? As bad as you are, you wouldn't think of such a thing. You're at least decent to your own children. So don't you think the God who conceived you in love will be even better?

—Jesus to his disciples, Matt 7:7–11 MSG

Most of what I have learned about *asking* prayer has come the hard way—through raw lived experience. I have a strong memory of a street in the center of Geneva, Switzerland. Our Australian family was touring northern Europe by car, pulling a camping trailer. In the rain of a very wet summer, and with only a few minutes before shops closed for the lunch hour, we were searching for that extra long parking spot we needed for the camping trailer so we could stop and buy food, see the sights, and visit Calvin's church. It was a destination of special significance for the son to whom we had given the great man's name. So I prayed for a parking space!

That was a new experience for me. I was not in the habit of asking for such things. In everyday life, if I am running late and cannot find a place to park, I blame myself for not leaving enough time to search for one or not checking out the location or the parking app beforehand. In a rare emergency, I have asked God for personal physical needs, recovery from a cold, or a good night's sleep when I had a demanding day ahead but justified it as an exception. To make it a habit seemed the worst kind of petulant demanding, expecting God to be at my beck and call.

As it happened, an extra long space did appear at that moment in Geneva, though we nearly knocked a motorcyclist off his bike in our sudden move to commandeer it! In the days that followed, my spontaneous request to God for a parking spot became the trigger for a new look at *asking* prayer. I discovered I had been making a big distinction between what I considered God's spiritual realm, where of course I could expect his help, and the physical world I knew and lived in. I realized that when I prayed for an everyday concern such as a parking space, I was uncomfortable because I felt I was crossing between the two spheres and expecting God's help in something I should take care of myself. Moreover, it seemed very selfish.

THE GOOD FATHER WELCOMES OUR ASKING

Thinking of ourselves as daughters or sons invited to live in God's house with gracious access to the Father challenges this view. The Good Father *wants* to give good gifts to his children, so we should approach him without hesitation and ask through prayer. Of course, prayer includes many other aspects, but at its most basic it is, as Jesus told his followers, the cry of a child to their father. That seems almost too simple, but as I read the Gospels, I am confronted by how many times Jesus instructs his followers to *simply ask*.

In his face-to-face encounters with people, Jesus was particularly insistent that they *ask* for help if that was what they were seeking. To the man who had been sick for thirty-eight years and waited in vain by the pool in Jerusalem for healing, Jesus said, "Do you want to get well?" (John 5:6). It seems a silly question to address to an invalid, but we understand it to mean that even when the Master of the universe is before you, you are to just ask in faith. The crippled man had given up hope, and Jesus, ever the perceptive healer and teacher, was prompting hope in him as well as faith, perhaps challenging him to rise out of a resigned acceptance of his situation (John 5:1–15).

On another occasion, Jesus stopped as he passed blind men by the side of the road. They were calling out to him, so he said, "What do you want me to do for you?" "Lord," they answered, "we want our sight." And he gave it to them (Matt 20:29–34).

Earlier, when his disciples had asked him to teach them to pray, the prototype he gave them was all about asking. He prefaced it by saying, "This is your Father you are dealing with, and he knows better than you what you need. With a God like this loving you, you can pray very simply. Like this: Our Father in heaven . . ." (Matt 6:8–9a MSG).

This model prayer goes on to include asking for big important things, like God's kingdom to come on earth but also for the necessary, ordinary things: "Give us today our daily bread." We are encouraged to ask simply, just like that.

And many do. Even in Australia, surveys show that most people claim they pray at least sometimes. Many say they pray regularly. I have always dismissed such praying as a lazy going to God with a list of wants, a string of "give-me" requests that seem rather presumptuous.

True, if we have a high view of God, the Creator of the universe, the One who inhabits the heavens, whose power is far beyond anything we can even dream of, we should definitely hesitate to call him up like a genie in a bottle. But if we know God as the *Good Father* and he has invited us to enjoy being back home, this is a welcome invitation. We can come to the Source of all life and goodness in the simple expectation that the One who loves us will hear and answer. We ask simply in prayer because Jesus wants us to grasp how God our Father is so much more loving, more responsive, more understanding than even the best of human fathers.

SO WHY DON'T WE DO IT—SIMPLY ASK?

In ordinary things of life, many of us, for what seem good reasons, hesitate to just ask like that. As I have examined my praying practice, I have been startled to discover that each of these "hesitations" which I thought came from a place of humility, is countered by Jesus' words as he calls his followers to depend on the Father in the same way he did. Understanding these hesitations can help us dismantle barriers to fully entering into everything the Good Father wants to give us, now we have come home.

Hesitation 1: We Feel Unworthy, Insignificant, or Our Requests Too Trivial and Selfish

In 1942 under attack in the Philippines, an army chaplain is reported to have said, "There are no atheists in foxholes." It was the chaplain's experience that even those who had previously declared they had no faith in God, when facing acute danger, cried out to God for help.

In a crisis when there is nothing we can do, we, too, pray foxhole prayers. A few years ago, when my husband was diagnosed with cancer, we followed the best of medical advice and treatment and thought that was the right way to tackle the crisis. But a lot of foxhole prayers also rose from our family and friends. With a good outcome to the cancer, I suspect most of us have returned to trying not to bother God over lesser issues. Our general experience of life is that the important people get attention and get it first. The rest of us are further down the pecking order. So why should we worry the high and holy God about our little problems? That is being lazy. And anyway, we'll only make fools of ourselves by presuming we are important!

Not so! Martin Luther's sixteenth-century Reformation was partly to help ordinary believers understand they, too, had direct access to God. So he says this to them:

> [God] knows that we are timid and shy, that we feel unworthy and unfit to present our needs to God. . . . We think that God is so great and we are so tiny that we do not dare to pray. . . . That is why Christ wants to lure us away from such timid thoughts, to remove our doubts, and to have us go ahead confidently and boldly.[1]

But even if we acknowledge that God is concerned for us personally and that we have received the Father's unconditional acceptance, we may still feel as if wanting something for ourselves, making a request for an everyday item, is too much. We may not yet value ourselves as God does. We may not see that whatever is given to us, undeserved as it may be, is rightfully for God's delight as well as for ours because the Good Father loves to give to his children. When in Africa I have talked to desperate refugees fleeing danger with their family, I have seen that the deepest pain for a parent, more than their own hardship, is not being able to provide for their children. Similarly, our joy and satisfaction in receiving from the Father is also a delight to him. We cannot repay him. Expressing gratitude and showing similar generosity to others are the only ways we can give back to this openhanded Giver.

If we nevertheless are still concerned that everyday requests are trivial or mundane, not part of asking prayer, it is worth looking again at Jesus' model prayer. After we have prayed for God's kingdom, Jesus tells us to say,

1. As quoted in Stott, *Sermon on the Mount*, 184.

"Give us today our daily bread" (Matt 6:11). *Bread* can cover a lot of things. It can be metaphorical or practical, spiritual or mundane, but the key word here is *daily*. It translates a rare Greek word which long perplexed translators. Relatively recently, however, it was discovered written on an ancient scrap of papyrus against an item on what turned out to be a shopping list.[2] The word Jesus used has a very ordinary, necessary, down-to-earth feel about it.

Daily also reminds us of the way God gave manna to the Israelites as they traveled the long years from slavery in Egypt through the desert to their promised land. God's instructions were explicit: collect the dew-like substance for your meals every morning (daily) because it will not keep till the next day (except for the Sabbath). People learned that the manna was always reliably there, but they had to collect it *daily*, reminding them they were dependent on God's provision, even if it became a bit boring after years in the wilderness! Similarly, the promise is that we can count on the Good Father wanting his daughters and sons to have daily what they need for survival, to have enough of the basics.

This is not asking for luxury or frivolous things but everyday necessities, the simplest things in life. And presumably more than food. Agnes Sanford writing on prayer uses the example of someone desperately needing shoes. She put it this way:

> How strange it is that people who fear to do this [pray for the needed pair of shoes] do not hesitate to pray for the most difficult objective of all, such as the peace of the world or the salvation of their souls. If they have so little confidence in prayer that they do not dare to test their powers of contacting God by praying for the easy thing, it is probable that their cosmic intercessions are of little force.[3]

Do we dutifully pray for what we consider of world importance but think our little things are beyond God's notice? Not so. The Good Father knows in his sovereignty what we need and what is best for us right now.

Hesitation 2: Alternatively, We Are Confident That God Knows What We Need for Our Good and Have No Need to Ask!

When people try to live without reference to their Father God, what they miss out on is the relationship. Giving and receiving is part of any valued

2. Barclay, *Matthew*, 216–17.
3. Sanford, *Healing Light*, 8.

friendship, and it is that give-and-take with us that God desires most—a reciprocal relationship.

Reciprocal means that on our part we must also give. Some of us fear being obligated or dependent, and that may also hold us back from *asking* prayer. The truth is we *are* obligated, just by being created and loved. We teach our children to say *please* and *thank you* so that they do not thoughtlessly take what they have received for granted, or treat it as a right that cannot be denied. Similarly, *please* and *thank you* need to be built into our daily relationship with God. Two simple ways to acknowledge this are by giving thanks for a meal, enjoying all we have been given, and at the end of the day, reflecting on God's companionship and support before we relax into his gift of sleep. This applies of course to the bigger things in life too.

Another way that Jesus makes asking prayer normative is his story of the widow who pestered a judge to get the justice she needed. Jesus actually described what she did as *hassling, badgering* the judge! That is what he is telling his followers to do—hassle God, always pray, and never give up (Luke 18:1–8). Why, if this Good Father is so ready to give to us, should we pester him? Just as Jesus asked the man by the pool and the blind beggars to put into words what they wanted, so repeated, concrete asking shows we are invested in the specifics of our prayer.

Jesus is also teaching, as he often does, by contrast. If a *bad* judge gives to the widow what she needs because of her pestering, how much more will the *good* God give wisely and well. Some of us who have been pestering God for a long time for a family member or about a persistent problem need to hear again Jesus' teaching: "Always pray and never give up." Faith and hope in a Good Father can keep us holding on for an answer.

Hesitation 3: We Are Afraid to Ask Because the Answer Might Be "No"

This is a very real fear. Going out on a limb, making a major faith request, is a dangerous adventure which might fail. Even in the biggest traumas when we are most desperate—the threatened death of a loved one, the depths of depression, or the loss of our job—we are often afraid to pray specifically in case the answer is no. We fear a no may mean we never dare to ask in faith again.

When I mention publicly that my husband and I had many years of praying for a child and know the disappointment of not falling pregnant, I am often asked by childless couples to pray for them. Frequently I find they have never asked God specifically for the gift of a child. F. B. Meyer is reported to have said, "The greatest tragedy of life is not unanswered prayer, but unoffered prayer." Why have these couples not asked? Why have they not been more direct in their request to a loving, Creator God? Some confess that they are afraid that if they are too definite in their prayer and no child comes, God's "No" will cause them "to lose their faith." What is this faith that they are afraid to lose? Faith in their personal worthiness? Surely that is not fully appreciating the nature of the Good Father who wants only the best for us and loves giving to us.

In these circumstances, and with their agreement, we do pray very specifically for a child. We are putting our trust in the loving Father who will walk with them through the consequences of whatever comes next in their lives—baby or no baby. It may take time for a yes to become apparent, as it was for us, but even if it is finally a no, that does not mean they are not loved or have not asked rightly.

It is a similar act of trust when we pray fervently for a person to be healed. I remember as a pastor visiting a woman who was terminally ill and discovering that her praying friends would not countenance her husband calling in the family to say goodbye. The pray-ers told her that to do this would indicate a lack of faith that God would answer their desperate prayers for her recovery. She did die, but before that, she suffered several lonely weeks not able to say what she wanted to her family. Her husband also suffered a long period of regret afterwards, as well as his grief in her loss. I came to see that if God was saying no to the prayer for her healing, you could not blame her lack of faith nor that of her supporters. A kind of faith that depends on always getting what we pray for is not true faith. It is not faith in a loving God who knows best. We can trust our Good Father.

When I wrestle with texts that sound like Jesus is saying God always gives us what we ask for, I go back and read Heb 11 again. This great recitation of faith heroes concludes with a list of not-so-good outcomes—flogging, being sawn in two, killed by the sword, wandering in the desert. These heroes who lost their lives, whose prayers for survival were not answered in the positive, are also commended for their faith though they did not receive the ending they prayed for. We are surrounded by a great cloud of these faithful witnesses.

Hesitation 4: We Think the World Should Not Run on Miracles but on the Natural Principles God Created

If we have been prompted by Jesus' teaching to ask simply for more, there is still one part of his teaching that may offend us. Should we, as he suggests, expect to move mountains by praying? Even allowing that his words (reported in Matt 21:20–22 and Mark and Luke) are meant as a metaphor or hyperbole to make the point (not an uncommon practice for this teacher), faith to move mountains is a big ask. And if we have tried, it is likely we have failed. Our expectation is that the world does not normally work like that: creation principles of gravity and inertia usually apply! God has also given us the knowledge and services of gifted professionals, including scientists and engineers. In the case of mountains of healing, we could add doctors or psychiatrists to that list!

Maybe we have also been disturbed by the audacity of people praying for things in a demanding tone of voice as if the louder or more definitely they ask, God is obliged to grant the request, suggesting that the faith of such people tips over into faith in faith alone—that is, the harder (or louder) you believe, the more likely you are to receive. This leaves no room for the wisdom of the divine Giver who may bestow patience rather than healing. Or provide insight into how to tackle a problem rather than expecting you to pursue an easy or an instant way out.

Nevertheless, Jesus' instruction to ask for anything and everything is challenging. It makes us consider if we are asking enough. Are we making the most of having come home to a loving Father? And how do we combine that with the skills we and others have been given and developed?

One place to start is to bring to the *asking* prayer a listening posture. It is a two-way conversation. Our asking reveals what is most important to us in our relationship with our Good Father, but the Father usually has something to say too. We must welcome and be open to that. In listening, we may identify the root of our hesitation is that we do not want to be dependent on God.

OUR PRESSING DESIRE TO RUN OUR OWN LIVES

This hesitation—indeed, all our hesitations about just asking for what we need—may be a rationalization arising from a bigger issue: our desire to be independent of God. The Genesis origin story illustrates that human beings have had this impetus to be independent right back in the Eden garden. It has never disappeared. Listening as the first step in our prayer conversation with God will probably reveal it in us too.

Moreover, living in a Western society that glorifies independence and self-sufficiency, we are likely to experience this resistance most acutely. We have been taught that independence is a sign of maturity and strength, that it is childish to need to be constantly rescued or go running to a protector every time something goes wrong. Sure, we expect God to be here in the big catastrophes that naturally overwhelm us. We cry out from our "foxhole" when the bushfire surges, or the earthquake devastates, or our health is suddenly threatened. The rest of the time we think we should be managing on our own. We say, "God helps those who help themselves." We believe also that this is a healthy aspiration to have for our children. If once they were adults they continued to be dependent on us, we would be disappointed. We consider it should be like that with God too.

Later we will examine more directly this Western disease of individualism, but here, looking at asking prayer, we see Jesus directly contradicts this attitude in very plain words. He uses a picture of a fruit-bearing grapevine—a common sight on Mediterranean hillsides. "I am the vine; you are the branches. . . . If you remain in me and my words remain in you, ask whatever you wish, and it will be done for you" (John 15:5, 7). The branches of the vine, even the smallest ones, have life because they are part of the grapevine. Sap, with its sugars, hormones, and water, comes from the roots, through the vine, to the branch and produces the fruit. *Asking* prayer is our attachment to the source of life because Jesus has chosen us, invited us into him, the vine. "You did not choose me, but I chose you and appointed you so that you might go and bear fruit—fruit that will last—and so that whatever you ask in my name the Father will give you" (John 15:16). We and our requests are wanted, but there is a very strong condition attached: we must, like a branch, be connected to the vine, drawing what we need from it and not finding it solely from within our own resources.

Each of our protests about praying, and especially our overriding desire to be independent, is a failure to fully appreciate what it has meant to come home to God. The Father has sought us and found us, so of course he will listen to our pleas for help. Moreover, a big God cannot be overloaded. He handles whatever we ask, personalizes the response, encourages us when the answer is not what we are expecting, all this for the very good reason that this Good Father loves us, knows what is best for us, and wants to give to us. We can trust that love. Even in the blackest disappointment God is there with us, loving us constantly, teaching us through the "No!" as well as the "Yes!" But we only find that out when we take the risk of asking.

The best model for asking prayer is Jesus himself. In the Gospels we see his own straightforward requests to the Father—demonstrating their partnership. Before selecting his disciples, or multiplying bread to feed five thousand, or healing the man who was deaf and dumb, or sending his followers the promised gift of the Holy Spirit, he prays. At Lazarus's tomb, he prays. And the night before his death in his vulnerable and lonely Gethsemane vigil, he prays.

EXPERIMENT WITH ASKING PRAYER

P. T. Forsyth has said, "Prayer is for the religious life what original research is for science."[4] We can think of asking prayer as how we experiment, how we test the God connection and intention in our everyday lives. I embrace that, not just because my husband is an agricultural scientist for whom experiments are the way to advance knowledge and grow better crops but because through prayer I am learning more about God's view of this world and my part in it. It is how I am discovering if I am asking for enough, or if there is more that could be mine because of my connection to the Father. It is responding to Jesus' invitation to depend on him in all of life's activities.

We know that prayer includes many actions—praising, adoring, confessing, worshiping, listening, contemplating—but we are focusing here on *asking*. So I have a suggestion: experiment in *asking* prayers. Read the Gospels and bring them into your daily life. Notice what catches your attention as you read. If it is something that Jesus promised his disciples, ask it for yourself. If it is a command, ask God to help you obey and observe the outcome. Write the details down against the day's date and record what happens. Make notes of what you are learning in this experiment in prayer: about the Good Father, his connection to you, and the world you live in.

The psalmist reminds us to watch, waiting expectantly (Ps 5:3b). Last year in my devotional time I spent the twelve months just listening to the Father through the psalms.[5] As I read back through my jotted notes, I am amazed at the rich wisdom this Host of the universe gave me, inviting me to live in his house, enjoying its provision and security (Ps 23:6).

4. Forsyth, "Prayer and Its Importunity," 8.
5. I used Peterson's *Praying with the Psalms*.

Jesus' illustration of the vine and the branches includes another condition to our asking: we are to ask *in his name* (John 14:13–14, 16:23–24). How can we do that? Only by learning to hear his response to our asking. It is my testimony that there is so much more to know and experience in being at home with the Good Father. But we must be open to it, simply ask for it, and experience his reply.

Does that sound too easy? Yes, there is another dimension to this *asking* prayer—one I had to learn from stretching experience. I tell that story in the next chapter.

RESPONDING

- Ask God for the practical things you need right now. If that is too uncomfortable, ask God to show you why you hesitate and what to do about that.
- Experiment with *asking* prayer, noticing how the Good Father is working in your life. Talk to God about your reaction when he occasionally says no.
- Someone has said, "Never doubt in the dark what you know in the light." When you are in a dark place, what will be your light-filled reminders of God's faithfulness?

5

Please Rescue Me

Father, if you are willing, take this cup from
me; yet not my will but yours be done.

—Jesus in Gethsemane the night before his death, Luke 22:42

In 2009 I faced a precarious situation in South Sudan, causing me to cry out for God's protection. It was my third visit to South Sudan, and I was teaching in a theological seminary in the small town of Melut on the White Nile. This northernmost part of the country is where the much-valued oil reserves are located and so is of strategic importance. Internal fighting has long plagued South Sudan, and it had broken out again; an army was headed in our direction, presumably to take control of the oil riches. To leave Melut and escape for home I had to take a slow, hazardous journey through multiple roadblocks to Malakal, the regional center, and then a flight on a United Nations plane further south to the capital, Juba, with its international connections.

However, we soon heard that the combat troops had already reached Malakal, and the UN staff had been withdrawn. With them had gone the plane that was my escape. But we could not stay where we were; everyone needed to evacuate the college. The first day, we made the overland trip to the regional capital surprisingly safely, only to sit for two days in the office of a small local airline hoping for a flight further south. I was promised a seat on the first plane out, but throughout those two days, local "heavies" came and went into the office, clearly hoping one way or another to obtain one of those seats for their own escape. On the third day, a plane did come, but it was not until I had boarded it that I could feel confident I would leave and receive what I was fervently asking God for—a miracle to get safely out of the war zone.

Wrestling in prayer for my own safety had begun in earnest two weeks before, when the fighting first came near our college. This part of the back-story is best told in real-time excerpts from my emails back to Australia:

Melut, March 2

Dear friends and family,
I have a window of opportunity to send this email via a temporary computer link. It is the first internet access we have found in the ten days since we left Juba. The last five days we haven't even had phones working, so we have felt very cut off. . . .

Tuesday was the most dramatic day. About 9:30 a.m. I was sent a message to immediately suspend class and send everyone to their huts. Apparently, there was an uprising in the army in Malakal (the regional capital), and word has come that a renegade officer and his people are heading in our direction. We still don't know how serious the threat is. There was some shooting, and we could see army movements on the Nile from our location along the only road into town. However, the nearby UN base was very active, and they kept us informed of what was happening.

Later that day we were able to resume class when it was clear that the government had rushed reinforcements to the oil-related airfield about an hour away, strengthened the guard around the commissioner's house next to us, and stationed troops at the port on the Nile and in the town. Things were tense for a couple of days and the soldiers clearly seen, but they returned to their bases when the rebel officer gave himself up to the UN and was spirited away. The road from Malakal has been closed for some days and supplies of fruit and charcoal and eggs are scarce, but we couldn't have left even if we had wanted to, as that road is our only way out and there are no boats on the river. A week later and we wouldn't have been able to come in either, so the timing was just right for me to arrive and teach these two weeks. Westerners wouldn't have necessarily been a target, but fighting in the past has killed pastors and burned down churches, so everyone here is apprehensive.

When I arrived two weeks ago, I found I had a second class to teach, so every day I am at it from 8:30 to 3:30 with a stop for breakfast at 10:30, a cup of tea at 2:00 p.m., and the second and main meal of the day at 4:30. Then I prepare for the next day. But I'm really enjoying getting to know the students, hearing their stories, and teaching them slowly and simply as I find the right level to aim at. They are very appreciative that I have come back. The Australian engineer of seventy years and many skills who is with me has had a long association with Sudan but not been to Melut before. He has been good company. . . .

In the wide range of things the principal has to do, I see my father in his years as a theological college principal. But last Thursday it was his wife who was hauling twenty-liter water containers to our building for us to wash with. I don't think my mother ever had to do that! . . .

We now have a new latrine with a proper lid and full-height privacy protection. The brush fence shower screen has a new hole in the end wall so the water can be turned on and off from inside instead of having to reach up on the tank stand. Basic conditions obviously, but it is certainly a privilege to be part of training the first cohort of South Sudan, four-year-degree trained pastors from four denominations. They should graduate this year.

The plan is still for the engineer and me to leave here next Monday. There are almost no river boats now, so it means a day of bumping along in a taxi first then a bus on a truck chassis down the road to Malakal. The next day we expect to get to Juba by World Food Program plane, and I'll be in Uganda by Thursday.

Stuck in Malakal, March 10

Tuesday afternoon. The engineer and I arrived safely in Malakal after a harrowing journey from Melut on Sunday, and we spent yesterday trying to find a way to get to Juba for our connecting international flights. Since the fighting here last week, all foreigners but a few dedicated missionaries have left, and so all flights except military ones are suspended, including the UN one we were scheduled to fly out on.

Promised a flight today, we borrowed money from local missionaries to buy tickets and then spent five hours in a dust storm waiting for a plane that could not land. It turned back to Juba. We are promised a seat on tomorrow's one, but who knows? They normally only fly Tuesdays and Fridays. The alternative is a several days' journey by boat and overland to Juba. But if I don't get there tomorrow, I'll miss my onward connections. It is my fervent prayer that we will get on that promised twelve-seater plane tomorrow.

We are comfortable enough, returning from the airport each day to the missionary guest house where we are well looked after, and the young ex-pats here enjoy the extra company. Please join me in praying that we make progress tomorrow.

Safe in Juba, March 12

Now, dear friends, you can send up a cheer on our behalf! We have made it to Juba! We are greatly relieved to be here safely, and now we are going out to eat as we haven't had money for food for a few days.

Much prayer went up on our behalf here and from you in Australia over the past two days. Interestingly, I have been reading a book on prayer, which has a lot to say about waiting on God and asking directly, believing in faith that God wants only the best for us. Of course, sometimes the answer is no, *and we have to accept that. I was very aware when we left Malakal that the local people cannot leave, and the long-term missionaries choose not to. The local pastors I was teaching are particularly vulnerable. What right do I have to pray for a special rescue from God? Perhaps God should answer* no *to me in these circumstances.*

But this time God did say yes and answered first with a surprisingly safe overland trip, then the little twelve-seater that finally arrived out of the sky at 3:00 p.m. today and rumbled back to Juba by 5:00 p.m. We had spent six hours at the airport waiting for it yesterday and another six hours today. But it came. We were the first Westerners to get out of Malakal since the fighting began. An answer to prayer? Once we were strapped into our seats and the plane started taxiing, my tears of gratitude (and relief) flowed.

Tonight, I was reflecting on Heb 11—the chronicle of heroes who have lived (and died) by faith. This episode in my life was calling for that kind of faith and fervent prayer. Yet our temporary predicament seems so petty compared with that of the South Sudanese. The conflict has disrupted all the aid programs they depend on. The fighting is right in the city and affecting everyone. And they have seen the foreigners able to flee.

Yesterday evening we joined the open-air meeting at the local Malakal stadium called by the churches to pray for their predicament. Never have I been at a prayer meeting like that! How they long for peace and the keeping of the recent promises made to South Sudan. How they pray for protection. And for courage to stand up for their faith. They are the Heb 11 heroes, not us. But did we, and even they, have a right to expect God's protection? Nevertheless, I am sure we are always invited to ask our Father for protection.

THE SEQUEL

For the local people, the fighting did not stop. It has gone on for many more years and left most of the population of Malakal still living in makeshift refugee camps or out in the open under the sparse shade of thorn trees. Women have continued to be raped and boys stolen for army recruitment.

The fighting eventually reached the town of Melut, and the Bible college was sacked. All the facilities built over years were destroyed and left to rot on the hard-baked soil. The college has disappeared. God rescued us but not those we left behind with no option to flee. All of us were praying, praying, praying. Who was I to ask for special protection? I still wrestle with it, perhaps with survivor guilt, yet we are encouraged by the Scriptures, and especially by Jesus, to simply ask to be rescued.

HELP-ME-LORD PSALMS

After my experience in South Sudan, I keep noticing how many Old Testament psalms are desperate "Please rescue me" SOS calls to God. Psalm 3 is a good example. King David is fleeing from a son who is trying to wrest the kingdom from him and cries out,

> Arise, LORD!
> Deliver me, my God!
> Strike all my enemies on the jaw;
> break the teeth of the wicked.
> (Ps 3:7)

Some years into our marriage with no baby making an appearance, my husband and I were crying out to God for a child. The Good Father answered with a son, and we named him Matthew, a "gift from God." There is biblical precedent for this kind of prayer,[1] but it is not everybody's experience that God answers in the way they are hoping. Likewise, not all of us are in immediate physical danger like David, needing to be protected from the sword and seeing a strong divine response. And not everyone asking

1. 1 Sam 1:10.

for protection is rescued. Many of Jesus' chosen twelve apostles lost their lives spreading the good news, as did Stephen and Paul, whose stories we know from the book of Acts. There have been unnamed others seemingly abandoned since.

In addition to death or torture threats, our most poignant cries for help are likely to be for fractured family relationships—more heartfelt and persistent than even cries for physical rescue. Yet answers are often slow in coming. No parent wants to give up on their child, but parents can tire of praying for their wandering son or daughter or fear it shows lack of faith to keep raising it with God. One mother asked me, "How long should I go on pestering God about my child? It is dominating my prayers, and maybe I am not believing God will bring her back." The multiplicity of David's pleading psalms, just like Jesus' repeated instructions to "simply ask," reassure us that we can ask many times, trust many times, and know we are heard each time. Our lives—with God and with our children—matter. The answer may not be a sudden change in the one prayed for but a fresh supply of wisdom, of patience and understanding, and perhaps even forgiveness in the one who prayed. Most importantly, faith and trust in the Good Father teach us determination and perseverance to keep the channels of connection open with those we love.

PSALM 23

The rescue psalm we know best uses the imagery of a shepherd to reassure us of God's individual response to our needs. It is not a picture of an Australian sheep farmer whistling his dogs to round up a large mob of sheep and herd them between dusty paddocks or to the shearing shed. It is a more intimate Middle Eastern one. The shepherd knows each sheep in his small flock and leads them out each day to green pasture and quiet waters. Kenneth Bailey, a writer with extensive experience in the lands of the Bible, helps us understand the intimacy of this shepherd-sheep relationship.

> The shepherd walks slowly ahead of his sheep and either plays his own ten-second tune on a pipe or (more often) sings his own unique "call." The sheep appear to be primarily attracted by the voice of the shepherd, which they know and are eager to follow.[2]

2. Bailey, *Good Shepherd*, loc. 523.

He goes on to describe how many shepherds mingle their sheep, coming together while they rest in the heat of the day or by a water source. But when it comes time to move on again, the shepherds call their own sheep out from the larger flock. Each sheep recognizes its shepherd's voice and follows.

In 2014 when we were traveling in Turkey (what is now Türkiye) for my husband's work, the Ps 23 shepherd scene was realized before our eyes. That year there was a small window of time when tourists could wander safely around the eastern area of the country, bounded by strongly defended borders with Iran, Syria, and Iraq. More recently the overflow of the war in Syria, and the Turkish government's fear of Kurdish resistance, have made it a doubtful tourist destination. But that year we were there.

My husband and his plant scientist colleagues know this area as a center of origin of several major food plants, especially chickpea and wheat. The focus of their research is to increase productivity of these species. Undomesticated examples of the precious forbears of modern crops have survived on slopes too steep for systematic cropping, and these agricultural sleuths can spot them at a distance! Scientists breeding improved cultivars and maintaining seed banks for the future consider these wild plants very valuable for introducing new productivity characteristics into the modern crops, including resistance to disease or pests. It is remarkable that even after the more than ten thousand years since wheat was domesticated, specimens of the original wild types are growing in such areas season after season, undisturbed by ploughing.

As we traveled east, the plant scientists were noticeably excited each time they spotted a wild chickpea or wheat plant. Photos were taken and notes made. Then, as we were admiring the beautiful green rolling green hills we were passing through, one colleague who had grown up in this part of the world suddenly exclaimed, "See these hills? We have a poem about shepherds on hills like these." "Yes," my husband and I replied in unison, "we know it. The LORD is my shepherd. . . . He makes me lie down in green pastures." For the first time we were seeing in real life a version of what Ps 23 describes. Out on these hills Kurdish shepherds were "minding" their sheep. It was not a safe area. Manned watchtowers at frequent intervals on the ridge immediately south of the road we were traveling marked the border, first with Syria, then Iraq. A strongly guarded crossing into Iran lay just ahead. The hazards may have been somewhat different in the psalmist's day, but just as then, the lives of shepherds and their sheep continued in the midst of danger.

We could see, for example, after the winter cold, the sheep were being taken up to newly green higher pastures and carefully guided along paths to avoid precipices. The shepherds had formed ponds along fast flowing streams of snowmelt so fussy sheep (who will not drink moving water) could get what they needed. And the very pregnant and young sheep were being given extra protection by a temporary fence. The animals that had had enough to eat were lying down in the green pastures to digest their fill. In the distance we could even make out the narrow gorges the shepherds and sheep had to file through, gorges where any sudden rise in water from storm or snow melt would threaten their passage.

Suddenly, the comfort of Ps 23 came alive for us. The sheep could trust the shepherd's care and knowledge of where their water, food, and safety would come from. They would be led to the higher summer pastures on well-marked paths. And all this bounty was provided in the presence of enemies. No wonder it has become a favorite psalm, not just for shepherd David but for many of us down through the centuries.

TURKEY RESONATES

Turkey has other biblical resonances and contemporary visual references to the Middle Eastern settings of the Old and New Testaments. On that journey to the east of Turkey, we had crossed the great rivers of Mesopotamia—the Tigris and the Euphrates—and photographed Mount Ararat of Noah fame. On previous visits, we had explored Cappadocia, where early Christians in times of persecution had been forced to hide, living in caves dug into the rock. And we had visited the ruins of Troy and Ephesus and some of the other seven cities of chapters 2 and 3 of the book of Revelation. We had even seen in Haran what supposedly was Abraham's cave, a site honored by Muslims. This country is also home to Constantinople (Istanbul), named after the first Christian emperor of the Roman Empire and host to early councils of the Christian church, as well as the ascendancy of the post-Roman Greek-speaking era of the empire.

But for Australians there is a more modern place of pilgrimage—Gallipoli in the west, on the Aegean coast. Our national folklore says that here Australia became a nation—resisting annexation as part of the British Army and demonstrating in blood and bravery our emerging national character.

Gallipoli for Australians is always solemn, but I remember that first visit well because it was where we heard the news of the birth of a new grandson. I sat on what is now beautiful lawn above the treacherous cliffs that withstood the Australian assault and phoned home to Perth to offer our congratulations and prayers for this new life. New life where blood has been shed has a theological resonance, especially for those of us who follow the one who gave his life in neighboring Israel. It is Jesus' blood shed for us in Jerusalem that opens the door to our relationship with the Good Father.

MORE PLEASE-RESCUE-ME PSALMS

When we read psalms begging for God's protection, we are invited to pray the same way. Ps 59, another example, begins,

> Deliver me from my enemies, O God;
> be my fortress against those who are attacking me.

The heading suggests that this early psalm was prompted by David as a young man being pursued by King Saul's soldiers. We can imagine the setting and read in 1 Sam 19 how God answered him.

When, in a later incident with another happy outcome, David's two wives were captured and his soldiers threatening rebellion, the Chronicler says that King David found strength (literally "strengthened himself") in the LORD his God (1 Sam 30:6), who gave him wisdom as to how to proceed. His Ps 13 might have been written at this time with the Amalekites the enemy. But danger also came in his life from King Saul and later from his own son Absalom. Its pattern of pain, prayer, and praise finds echo in my testimony after rescue in South Sudan.

> I've thrown myself headlong into your arms—
> I'm celebrating your rescue.
> I'm singing at the top of my lungs,
> I'm so full of answered prayers.
> (Ps 13:5–6 MSG)

But we know from experience that our prayers are not always answered quickly or in the way we expect. And what we are asking for may just be too dangerous for us. Under the heading of "Prayer in the Cosmic Setting," Dallas Willard argues, "We do not know enough, and our desires are not perfect enough for us to be given everything we want and ask for."[3] He then quotes C. S. Lewis's *God in the Dock*:

3. Willard, *Divine Conspiracy*, 263–64.

> Prayers are not always . . . "granted." This is not because prayer is a weaker kind of causality, but because it is a stronger kind. When it "works" at all it works unlimited by space and time. That is why God has retained a discretionary power of granting or refusing it.

Previous generations sometimes followed a declaration of future plans with *DV*, Latin for "God willing." This can be used as emotional protection in case God answers with a no. However, in its best sense, it is not lazy passivity but acknowledging God as the arbiter of what is good and expressing a desire to avoid hubris in running our lives. But God does not take away our capacity and responsibility for things that are under our control. Referencing the model the psalms give us, Willard offers this description of prayer: "Talking to God about what we are doing together."[4]

BEING SENSIBLE

Some Christians pray for safety before leaving on a long car trip. Statistically, it is the most dangerous way of traveling in Australia, so it makes sense, but it should not replace careful, wide-awake driving. Similarly, when I have visited countries known for major health risks, I have prayed for God's protection. But I supplement that with timely hand washing, teaching myself not to touch my face, eating and drinking only cooked foods and boiled water, and accepting all the available vaccinations as well as malarial prophylaxis. This is not just "God helps those who help themselves!" It is recognizing that the Father who rescues us has also given us health knowledge, proven routines, and sensible rules of living that we can put into practice to serve others better.

It is parallel to getting enough rest to function as the Creator intended. As the psalmist says,

> In vain you rise early
>   and stay up late,
> toiling for food to eat—
>   for he grants sleep to those he loves.
> (Ps 127:2)

Sleep is both a gift from God and fostered by good sleep hygiene. While acknowledging that there are health conditions that contribute to sleeplessness, for many years I have taught the theology of sleep as an

4. Willard, *Divine* Conspiracy, 267.

example of biblical theology applied to everyday life.[5] But more recently as I have aged, getting good quality sleep has become a problem, and I have had to embrace a combination of seeking medical therapy and bringing my anxiety about it to God, praying for his intervention. This is the great blessing of the relationship we are invited into by the Good Father.

JESUS IS OUR MODEL

We see the way Jesus related to God the Father throughout his earthly life, and it gives us even more reason to believe that the Good Father hears and welcomes our requests for help and protection. The answer may be wisdom about what to do next, or patience to wait for divine intervention—perhaps a wonderful surprise miracle—or sometimes, a "No."

In Gethsemane the night of his betrayal Jesus prayed to be spared the cross. He knew the answer must be no if he was to complete his mission, but the prayer expressed his relationship with the Father and his need at this crucial and difficult time for that intimacy. Please-help-me prayers need not be resignation or inertia but expressing a desire and deep dependency in that intimacy. Only a child has the right to pester their father for big or little things—only a God-botherer can ask for rescue—but we join a great cloud of witnesses testifying that God hears and answers, and there are glorious rescues. Or not. Why remains a mystery.

Meanwhile, the Good Father, the Giver of all gifts, has another one to give us. We will celebrate that next.

RESPONDING

- Do you have a favorite psalm? Remember the circumstances that made you love that psalm and ponder what you learned from that first experience. Maybe you understand more now than at the time you read or heard it.
- Have you ever prayed for physical rescue? Have you experienced survivor guilt? Did this build empathy in you? What are you doing with these feelings, good or distressing?

5. Turner, "Theology of Everyday Life."

- Picture what strengthening yourself in your Good Father relationship looks like in your life at the moment. Have you been talking to God about what you are doing together? What practical steps must you now take?

6

The Creator's Gift of Awe

The whole earth is filled with awe at your wonders;
where morning dawns, where evening fades,
you call forth songs of joy.
—David, Psalm 65:8

In our younger and more energetic days, my husband and I sought out trails to hike and vast scenery to experience in awe-inspiring wilderness, predominately in North America. Our highest peak was the fourteen-thousand-foot glacier-topped Mount Rainier near Seattle. Preparation for that included training in ice climbing skills—skills put to good use when I fell into a crevasse and used my ice axe to arrest my slide but had to be hauled out by those roped either side of me!

Before North America, my husband's nature playground was England's Lake District. We have walked there many times since, one summer taking some of our Australian grandchildren to experience its beautiful and fearful ridges so well known to their grandfather.

My peak awe experience was sighting Mount Everest from the base camp on the Chinese side. Its summit, so very recognizable in clear weather, is forbidding. Despite climbing many mountains in the past, including some with ice-topped peaks, we never aspired to tackle this highest one! Everest is magnificent, awesome to behold, but has "No!" written all over it. My lungs would never have let me conquer it, and I cannot imagine the devastating feeling, after spending years in preparation and months of training at altitude, of eventually having to turn back before reaching the top. We decided early it was better not to even try; its scale was beyond us. Yet it is that unobtainable height and ice that makes Everest so inspiring of awe! Awe that includes fear.

EXPERIENCING AWE

Awe is an emotional response to something beyond yourself. It is wonder, with a touch of an Everest kind of fear. It moves us *inwardly* stimulated by something *outside* of our control, and whatever stimulates awe in us—beauty, intricate design, vastness too great to encompass, a raging storm—its very detail or immensity has an edge of otherness. Whether big or small, it is too much for us. It takes us beyond ourselves.

In a Western world where the focus is on the individual and our hunger for love, we need awe to take us out of ourselves and our preoccupation with the inner life. That is why I believe the Creator gives us the gift of awe as well as the gift of love. We must receive it gratefully and embrace it.

The Covid-19 epidemic was when I first began thinking about awe. In Perth in 2020 we entered a lockdown that was relatively short and less restricted than in most places. Nevertheless, it became obvious that some people around us, especially those who lived alone, were finding the isolation particularly hard. So we invited our neighbors during that March's equinox to come out of their houses and gather on our front lawn because twice a year, at the spring and autumn equinoxes, we have a few days when the sun appears to set at the end of our east–west street over the nearby Indian Ocean. Sometimes it gives us a sky of red, sometimes just an orange ball sliding into the sea, but this Covid year we stood together "socially distanced" with drink in hand to watch it. The personal interactions were important during Covid-19 and the reason we got together, but I saw how greatly those conversations were enhanced in the presence of a glorious sunset. We began an equinox practice that we have continued each year since then. I have told this story before,[1] but I tell it again because this began my exploration of awe, especially awe shared with others.

For me, awe is best experienced in these big generous displays of nature. It might be a colorful sunrise or sunset, the sound of pounding waves on a rocky cliff, or a lightning storm out to sea, and these are one reason

1. Turner, *Finding Your Voice*, 81. Turner, "Turning Points in Contemplative Life."

we live where we live. But awe also describes occasions of small astonishing wonder. In the warm season each year my husband and I snorkel, watching the fish along the nearby limestone coastal reef. We delight in identifying them and anticipating what we will see in each month of summer. Being in the Indian Ocean is a daily activity, yet an unexpected spotting of a rare species or an enormous swirl of smaller fish brought up the coast on a warm current provokes awe.

THERAPEUTIC AWE

The value of going out into the natural world has long been acknowledged. In Japan it is known as "forest bathing," with claims it reduces blood pressure and stress and has cardiac benefits. More recently it has come to the attention of our frantic and fractured Western society through doctors using "nature prescribing" to get their patients into healing nature.

This therapeutic effectiveness has been demonstrated by scientific research, but how does it work? It seems that experiencing something bigger or more intricate than our worries—whether a forest, a wide landscape, or a delicate color or flower—shifts our focus from ourselves and brings a positive change of perspective. Similarly, rhythms of the rising and setting sun, the waxing and waning of the moon, the rolling over of the seasons, remind us that the larger world goes on, no matter our personal circumstances. When life events seem to be closing in around us, this is a great benefit.

Experiencing awe is more intense than just observing nature. Its presence is bigger (or more intricate) than anything we can do ourselves and so moves us emotionally. Californian psychologist Dacher Keltner is convinced by his team's research that experiencing spine-tingling awe is a great producer of happiness. His team defined awe as "the feeling of being in the presence of something vast and mysterious that transcends your current understanding of the world,"[2] and they collected 2,600 narratives of awe from across twenty-six countries. As expected, there was great variation in what stimulated awe for people, and it differed from culture to culture, especially when it was tinged with fear.[3] Keltner did not say so, but I wonder if we all have a creature's sense that there is someone who creates in more astonishing detail than we can even imagine. And that consciousness is given to us by our Creator, who was there before the beginning.

2. Keltner, *Awe*, 7.

3. Keltner, *Awe*, 9.

AWE HUNTING DAILY

In Australia, a TV program hosted by Julia Baird presented Keltner's work on cultivating wonder in everyday life. She highlights her own delight at the natural occurrence of ocean phosphorescence, crediting it with contributing to her recovery from personal trauma.[4] For the sake of our own well-being, she urges us to be daily "awe hunters" and suggests there are many surprises of awe to be found by those who go looking for them in the very small everyday things, even in our neighborhood.

This walk in nature is more than exercise, though we know that is good for us as well. It involves noticing, wondering, marveling at the complexity and power of what we observe. It can take us well beyond personal therapeutic value, even beyond a stimulus for worship, to something just as essential to human flourishing. Let me explain.

INTIMACY AND GOD'S OTHERNESS

We started this book with Jesus' story of the prodigal son's return and celebrated the delightful intimacy offered by the welcoming and forgiving Father when we come home where we belong. Then we explored what would happen next for a returned prodigal. He almost certainly would have hurts and scars that needed addressing and the opportunity to just ask his father for what he needed. On occasion his father would say no to his requests, and he would still be learning to trust that his father was good. As we shall see in the next chapter, this intimacy and healing are also available to hard-working older sons, if they only choose to come into the family circle.

But if we who live in individualistic Western societies concentrate only on our inward spiritual journey and personal privilege, we are in danger of reinforcing the worst of our self-focused culture. And contributing to its destructive tendencies. We need awe, whether arising from something small or large, but from outside ourselves and our introspection, to turn our attention to more than ourselves. We need the gift of awe to widen our horizon beyond ourselves and point to God—both Father and Creator.

The Scriptures hold the intimacy God lovingly offers his created people in tension with his might and power as Creator of the whole universe. Interestingly, after centuries of Enlightenment-stimulated science, the horizon of the universe we now can see is ever expanding as we explore it with

4. Baird, *Phosphorescence*.

telescopes and spacecraft. We know now there are vastly more stars than the ancients saw when they looked up at the skies and wondered. And we can only marvel at the intricacies and fine-tuning of the subatomic particles scientists are uncovering, or the fine balance of human biochemistry which takes researchers deeper and deeper into origins and first causes. But we still want to focus on ourselves and still seek to be in control!

So awe and reverence for God's creation provide balance to our tendency to be concerned only with the *self.* A God who is welcoming but cannot be limited by our minds or hearts is needed today more than ever. Even when we call him Father and relish that relationship, we must regard God not only as *close* but *other*, not to be taken for granted and certainly not to be boxed into our little consciousness. Our Creator is beyond us, outside of our passing systems and culture. Our Creator is a powerful *other*.

SELF-FOCUSED CULTURE

Many of us look back on the history of Western culture and rejoice that we have left behind the rigidity and restrictive identity roles of earlier times. Once we were defined by the family or class or nation into which we were born. That still applies in many cultures today, but now in the West we largely have the freedom to explore how God has gifted us. Thirty years ago, I had new opportunity to respond to God's call to pastor in a way not previously possible for women of older generations in my denomination. For my husband, freeing up of opportunities meant he could go to university and not leave school at fourteen for a sheet-metal apprenticeship, as his father and brother did.

But it is becoming increasingly obvious that this freedom, rather than being all good, is standing in the way of forming a secure, unambiguous identity in our society and robbing us of family and community cohesion in the process. Ordinary life is now so fluid and free of outside restraints that the search for identity becomes a prolonged lifelong struggle for many people, with unexpected personal consequences and a feeling of being unsupported along the way.

Observers blame this unlimited freedom to be and do what we like for the many woes of Western postmodern society—weakening of marriage and family ties, youth disillusionment, increasing rates of suicide, society fragmentation into left-right extremes, growing economic inequality, homelessness, and above all, loneliness. When we see these problems around us in our communities, even in our families, we feel helpless to turn the tide. And just going back to the old ways and culture probably will not work either.

Some claim that the problem is that we are lost in a morass of consumerism, chasing after money, sex, and power, and this explains our anxiety and fragmentation. These lures, however, are not new. It was against them that the early Christians developed vows of poverty, chastity, and humility. Richard Foster has written succinctly about the universal danger in all societies of money, sex, and power.[5] So also has Christian apologist Tim Keller, warning of the empty promises of these counterfeit gods of Western society.[6]

However, a more nuanced view of contemporary Western society is now needed. It will show that excesses in the arenas of money, sex, and power are not the cause of our current problems but some of the symptoms. They are external signs of the shift of more and more people to focus solely on discovering and uncovering their personal identity in order to live their best life, regardless of its effect on their relationships and responsibilities. They are ignoring, even exploiting, those around them in the search for their *self* and feeling little responsibility for contributing to others or making a better society. As a consequence, we are all the poorer emotionally and spiritually.

EXPRESSIVE INDIVIDUALISM

Recently, observers have begun calling this underlying *self*-only thinking in Western society not just individualism or even *hyper*individualism but *expressive* individualism.[7] They use this term to describe the values now taking hold and assert that self-expression has tipped so far in this direction that human relationships are being damaged.

In the term *expressive individualism*, we know what *individualism* means. It involves distancing myself from community and putting the focus primarily on me, myself, and I.[8] Everyone else is deemed irrelevant or of no concern to me. Someone recently argued in a local radio conversation, "How you choose to live doesn't affect anyone else." That clearly is not

5. Foster, *Money, Sex and Power*.
6. Keller, *Counterfeit Gods*.
7. For example, sociologist Richard Bellah.
8. The title of an insightful book by psychologist Arch Hart.

true but an indicator that such high value is placed in the *self*, that claiming its rights vigorously is a good that no one can argue against.

The adjective *expressive* asserts that the central human life task is to expose this essential *self*. For a person to be healthy, it is believed that their true self must be uncovered, acknowledged, and affirmed by others, overriding all other values and people in the process if necessary. No one should stop me doing this or try to persuade me otherwise! Sociologist Robert Bellah explains, "Expressive individualism holds that each person has a unique core of feeling and intuition that should unfold or be expressed if individuality is to be realized."[9] In popular speech this means, "You do you!"

This personal "buffered" *self* supposedly must have strong borders against the outside world, seeking to find its identity only internally by introspection and then given unhindered display. This *self* replaces the "porous" *self* which in previous understandings relied on and connected to community and family relationships for at least part of its identity.[10]

EXPRESSIVE INDIVIDUALISM OUTCOMES

In societies like ours, one manifestation of *expressive individualism* is the stress on exclusive ownership of one's own body. This may be a factor contributing to the increase in suicides, especially among young people. Choosing the drastic action of taking one's own life and disregarding the consequences for others implies that the personal right to exercise agency is more important than close relationships. In effect, this outlook says, "I am a piece of property that I own. Because I possess property rights to my*self*, I can dispose of my property as I see fit."[11]

Other trends—for example, the move towards unfettered use of abortion, the anxiety epidemic among teenagers, and a dramatic rise in the number of girls presenting with early onset gender dysphoria—have also been linked to an expectation that the only resources available to a person are to be found within the *self*, with no expectation of, nor desire for, help from a supportive family or community. And in return, no responsibility to the community or society as a whole.

9. Bellah et al., *Habits of the Heart*, 333–34.

10. *Buffered* and *porous* are terms used by philosopher Charles Taylor, quoted in Keller, *Making Sense of God*, loc. 1942.

11. David Brooks, "The Canadian Way of Death," *Atlantic Quarterly*, June 2023, as quoted in Kelly, "Comment Column."

Christians have long recognized the importance of the individual and their personal physical, emotional, and spiritual growth and have thus championed human rights, affirming that every person is created in the image of God and should be treated equally and sympathetically. As a consequence, Christians have historically led the way in establishing schools, hospitals, and social services deliberately targeted for those with fewer resources and power. But Christians also understand that we are created to live in community, made in the image of the three-in-one God. Our rights are tempered by obligation to both the divine and the human community. This means accommodating and serving others, giving as well as taking.

EVERYBODY WORSHIPS

The primary problem with expressive individualism, however, is that when identity is found solely in the *self*, *self* becomes the highest value. *Self* is what is worshiped. Novelist David Foster Wallace has warned,

> Everybody worships. The only choice we get is what to worship. And an outstanding reason for choosing some sort of god or spiritual thing to worship . . . is that pretty much anything else you choose to worship will eat you alive.[12]

Keller also recognized the significance of the shift in Western culture to a new form of individualism. His 2009 book on counterfeit gods was a philosophical view of Western society, but in 2016 he released *Making Sense of God*. In this more sociological approach focusing on the emerging trap of expressive individualism,[13] he says,

> In all former cultures, people developed a *self* by moving toward others, seeking their attachment. We found ourselves, as it were, in the faces of others. But modern secularism teaches that we can develop ourselves only by looking inward, by detaching and leaving home, religious communities, and all other requirements so that we can make our own choices and determine who we are for ourselves.[14]

This is why the gift of awe the Creator gives to people and societies is so essential for human flourishing. It is particularly important for a culture such

12. As quoted in Keller, *Center Church*, 34.
13. Hansen, *Timothy Keller*, ch. 17.
14. Keller, *Making Sense of God*, loc. 1953.

as ours which is so focused on the *self.* It serves as a corrective to the human desire to possess—whether money, sex, power, or whatever—because with awe, what we experience is outside of ourselves and bigger or more intricate than anything we can produce. Awe should also discourage us from being a consumer of nature and experiences as if we owned them. Our eyes and ears must shift from ourselves to our awesome Creator and call us to worship only God who is the ultimate glory.

GOD'S CATHEDRAL SHARED WITH US

One day as we hiked part of the Cape-to-Cape trail south of Margaret River in Western Australia, we sat and looked at the magnificent ocean vista. Below us, surfers were trying to master the famous left-hand break, and I found myself wondering if, long before humans discovered the pleasure of riding it, the Creator rejoiced when the surf was up. In the long history of the world, surfing with boards is a relatively recent ocean activity. However, the book of Genesis records that on the seventh day of creation, God enjoyed *all* he had created. The day of creation's completion became the rest of satisfaction and pleasure. Presumably, that included waves that one day would give these surfers the ride they were patiently waiting for out beyond the breakers!

I like to think of the created universe as God's cathedral—something even more substantial than the high-vaulted buildings through which talented human designers seek to construct awesome grandeur. The majesty of nature in sunset, storm, mountain, forest, ocean, or the intricacy of a flower or the human body—all that provokes awe in us, the Creator enjoys too in his cathedral. Awe is the way we can enter into it with him because he desires, it seems, the extra pleasure of sharing creation with us.

Enjoying nature is often thought of as a solitary activity, and no doubt there are times when its benefit to us is getting away from the pressures of people and tasks. But research indicates that sharing awe is important to its healing power. This includes sharing the enjoyment of beauty with its Creator. C. S. Lewis, moved by the beauty of colors and tastes, once speculated that even angels may not experience them as we do, and he comes to this conclusion: "I fancy the 'beauties of nature' are a secret God has shared with us alone. That may be one of the reasons why we were made."[15] We might

15. Lewis, *Readings for Mediation and Reflection*, 93.

dare to add to Gen 1,"In the beginning God created, *and desired to share with us*, the heavens and the earth."

WORSHIPING THE CREATOR

The psalms provide us with many examples of acknowledging the Creator and worshiping only him. Psalm 19 begins with the wonder of the created world.

> The heavens declare the glory of God;
>   the skies proclaim the work of his hands.

Many psalms like this bring God-perspective to humans who are inclined to either laud their own mastery of this world or wallow in despair at how we are making a mess of it.

Significantly, worship of the one, true, high, and holy God is very often linked in the psalms with his care for the people he has created. God's creative power and intimacy are combined. These poetic songs unite God's love with awe in his creation.

> When I consider your heavens,
> the work of your fingers,
>   the moon and the stars,
> which you have set in place,
>   what is mankind that you are mindful of them,
> human beings that you care for them?
> (Ps 8:3–4)

We see this also in Ps 136 with its chorus promising the Creator's forever-love for his people after every description of his work:

> Give thanks to the Lord of lords:
>   *His love endures forever.*
> to him who alone does great wonders,
>   *His love endures forever.*
> who by his understanding made the heavens,
>   *His love endures forever.*
> who spread out the earth upon the waters,
>   *His love endures forever.*
> who made the great lights—
>   *His love endures forever.*
> the sun to govern the day,
>   *His love endures forever.*

the moon and stars to govern the night;
His love endures forever.
(Ps 136:3–9)

Reading this psalm with its repetitive refrain always makes me smile. I remember an occasion when a leader asked us to read it aloud in unison but told us to save time by leaving out the repeated "His love endures forever." Yet that enduring love is the central point! It is the magnificent Creator who loves us! And he always has time to love.

THE FEAR IN AWE

Beauty, wonder, majesty, complexity are all positive words associated with awe, but any appreciation of awe must take into account that it can prompt the emotion of fear as well. The vigor of a thunderstorm, the roar of ocean waves and tides, the vastness of the sky in sunsets and sunrises, and especially the destructive energy of earthquakes and tsunamis all remind us of a creation big and beyond us. We know we cannot control its forces or domesticate it; nor should we try to tame it, nor ignore the God who created it.

In the apostle Paul's confronting words in the first chapter of Romans, there is a warning for today's Western culture: "For since the creation of the world God's invisible qualities—his eternal power and divine nature—have been clearly seen, being understood from what has been made, so that people are without excuse" (Rom 1:20). Nature's fearsome strength as well as its beauty is certainly experienced by everyone, but their sinful refusal to submit to God's sovereignty blinds many to its Creator, and they choose not to reverence him. Rather than letting the gift of awe prompt worship, humans construct pathetic substitutes, wooden images, or a *self* to worship instead! They will be held accountable for that alternative idol and draw to themselves God's wrath.

BOTH INTIMACY AND AWE

Keller subtitled his book on *Prayer* with *Experiencing Awe and Intimacy with God.* I treasure the reality that prayer brings together awe and intimacy when we relate to God as both Creator and Father. What a wonderful combination! This both/and is in the Lord's prayer too. "Hallowed be your name," it begins, honoring the mighty Creator before inviting us to ask our Father what we need for daily life.

My parents had four years of engagement before their marriage. So when in old age my mother was no longer able to communicate, my father got out all their letters to each other from their engagement separation that he had kept for nearly fifty years. Each day he read one to her as they enjoyed together the memories from their long, loving relationship. Then he typed the letters out, omitting what he called "the mushy bits," and distributed them to my brothers and me. It brought me a deeper appreciation of my parents but also of the privilege of being in conversation with another father, God my Father.

I also remember that my human father had such a high view of God's connection to him that he would never countenance resting anything on top of his Bible. He greatly valued the precious words from the God he knew intimately and reverently. Putting a Bible on the floor was an absolute no-no. When I was young, I did not appreciate this and thought it was almost superstitious. But I stopped putting my Bible on the floor when I began visiting Islam dominated countries. It is forbidden in Islam for the Qur'an to be put low; certainly it should not be rested on the floor. How much more for the Christian Scriptures with their words from the God who is both far and near, awe-creating and loving.

The apostle John begins his Gospel echoing the Gen 1 creative act of God—Father, Son, and Spirit—speaking the world into existence. "In the beginning was the Word, and the Word was with God, and the Word was God" (John 1:1). He then announces the very heart of his Gospel: this Word, this Son "from the Father, full of grace and truth" (verse 14) is the one we know as Jesus who came to live in human flesh and show us the power of love. Creative power and love were united from the very beginning because creation and intimacy are together in the Godhead, dwelling among us through Jesus.

CELEBRATING THE CREATOR'S GIFT OF AWE

There are many ways to worship the Creator and celebrate this gift of awe. There is the daily eyes-open awe walk already mentioned that we are urged to build into our lives. We need community awe experiences too, like walking together or sharing the sunsets with neighbors. Throughout the Old Testament, the nation God built through the descendants of Abraham were taught to celebrate the progression of the year and the agricultural seasons through their festivals. Giving thanks to the Creator and Sustainer of life lifted their agrarian eyes from their daily tasks and filled them with awe at the abundance of crops and herds. They were taught that all human life could come together in *shalom*, wholeness of body and spirit and world, working together in harmony in individual people and in the people of God. Their psalms celebrated the stars of the heavens too, and they acknowledged that their God, Yahweh, was not just a local deity but the Creator of all the world.

More recently, Celtic Christianity has continued this heightened awareness of the gift of creation and the awe it brings us, incorporating the rhythms of the seasons into the liturgy of their church communities.[16] These Christians call creation the fifth Gospel and look for "thin spaces" in nature where God seems more readily experienced. We can learn from them to value the strong connection between what is experienced in nature and worship of its Creator.

In Western society, we especially need the Creator's gift of awe to take us beyond our narrow inner world and our self-obsession. In the story of the return of the prodigal, we hear of the grace of recovered intimacy offered to the son who has come home. Awe inspiring creation is this other gift of grace to us, just as much as is the love of the Good Father. And as with the intimacy God offers, all we can do in the moment of awe is simply accept it with open hands and give thanks to the Giver of all good gifts.

But now we must go back to the thread running through this book, the story Jesus told because it has more to say to us. Jesus began with, "There was a man who had two sons." We must look not only at the prodigal but at what he tells us about the older son.

RESPONDING

- Have you thought of awe as a gift from the Creator? Try a daily "awe walk." The distance or location is not as important as getting out of the house or workplace if possible and into God's wide world. Notice your response to this gift of awe. Can you identify what leads you most easily to awe and wonder? It is not necessarily big—it may be small, something of intricate design. How can you integrate that into your worship? Ponder how you can share your awe experience with others.

16. Godwin and Roberts, *Grace Outpouring*, 149–52.

- Have you, like Celtic Christians, found places in your nature wanderings that connect you best to the Creator? Does thinking of these as "thin spaces" enabling your connection with God motivate you to use them more in worship and listening?
- Maybe psalms lauding the Creator especially resonate for you. Make a note of them and read them regularly.
- If your journey to explore your identity has been focused mainly on your inner *self*, how can you take into account the Creator's creation and wider grace to you? Consider where your family and community intersect with this journey.

7

That Older Son

The older brother became angry and refused to go in.
So his father went out and pleaded with him.
—Jesus continues his story, Luke 15:28

In a little mission church in Santa Barbara, California, I found my favorite representation of Mary Magdalene. The sculptor depicts Mary dropping her urn of ointment as she turns to look in wonder and awe at the risen Christ. She has come with other women to the garden tomb to anoint his body, not expecting to see him alive. But here he is!

Paired with the Magdalene statue in Santa Barbara is one of Jesus, burial clothes left behind in the tomb, extending his pierced hands to the startled woman who, until he says her name, does not recognize her beloved Master through her tears.

Mary Magdalene, too, was a prodigal. She, too, had come home to God through Jesus. Some commentators describe her as a former prostitute, and the way the sculptor has dressed her in his statue gives a hint of that. But the Gospels simply record her as a woman out of whom seven demons had come (Luke 8:2). Whatever it was that Jesus had delivered her from, she was a new woman, and on this resurrection Sunday she was entrusted with the astounding good news that Jesus had risen from the dead.

Not all of us have had a dramatic past, or fallen under demons like Mary Magdalene, or eaten with pigs like the prodigal. Some of us have grown up thinking of ourselves as *good.* Scrupulously obedient and hardworking, we (I identify with this) feel virtuous in our various roles and perhaps resent the attention prodigals receive. We may even be quick to see in the returning brother's groveling arrival evidence of his unacceptable character weakness!

Surprisingly at this point in the story, Jesus gives more words to the father's interaction with the older son than with the prodigal, but the hardworking older son does not present in a good light. He is adamant he does not want to have his life disturbed again by an errant younger brother; he has no wish to reconnect with him and certainly no desire to celebrate his homecoming. Why should he? The prodigal has devastated the family's finances, disturbed the rhythm of their lives, distressed his father (and presumably his mother), and now receives his father's open arms and ready forgiveness when he comes home with his tail between his legs. Then he gets a party!

Meanwhile, all this time the older son has faithfully continued his dutiful service and family support, probably keeping as far as possible from the household and certainly disowning his brother so as not to be associated with the family disgrace.

WILL YOU ALSO COME HOME?

In Jesus' story, the father leaves the party and goes out to the field to see why his other son has not joined the celebration. He says in effect, "Will you also come home?" But the bitter older son rejects both his father and his brother, responding in words like, "Why should I celebrate *your* son coming home? He doesn't deserve it! Look what trouble he's caused our family! I haven't received such generosity! It's not fair!"

We nonprodigals may not go so far in our bitterness, but nevertheless we can be tempted to think that focusing on dramatic returnees is too much! Soon everyone will think they, too, should be getting everything for nothing! We tell ourselves that someone has to work to keep the family and farm going and the finances coming in. Someone has to pay for the parties!

So we respond by laboring even harder and taking on more responsibilities to demonstrate we are needed. We deeply want our worth appreciated. We define ourselves as dutiful older brothers and sisters, choosing task and obligation over family relationships. And even over our relationship with God.

We are the poorer for it. We may not see what is happening, but we are downplaying the most important relationship in our life—with our Good Father. Older brothers and sisters need to come home to the waiting father as urgently as prodigals because the father's welcome to the good stay-at-home son is as important as the open arms to the prodigal. The father in Jesus' story did not let Middle Eastern dignity stop him running to welcome the prodigal son, and in going out to him in the field, he did a similar unexpected deed for the older one. He did not hesitate to leave the party to go and plead with him to come and join the family celebration. The older brother's retort about "this son of yours" shows he does not understand nor appreciate his father's longing heart for both his sons, nor his own emptiness. Despite his father reminding him the prodigal is *your* brother as well as *my* son, the older son's actions and words take him even further away from the offered family reconciliation.

Jesus addressed his parable to the superreligious practitioners of his day, the Jewish Pharisees. He also challenges people like me, and maybe you too. We older sons and daughters may never have strayed very far, so we do not know the joy of being a prodigal returning home nor the release from torment of a Mary Magdalene. However, though we would be horrified to be called Pharisees, we often find our faith journey with all its effort has become dry duty and a transactional relationship we take for granted. We hold our heads high and assert we do not have anything *big* to be forgiven for, so we do not savor the intimacy with God, Creator and Father, that we celebrated in earlier chapters. But there is a homecoming for us too because there is a loving Father!

Theologian Helmut Thielicke, writing about repentance from this New Testament story, notes that despite the older son's denials, we all have a longing for home with its warm acceptance, forgiveness, and love. "The ultimate secret of this story is this: There is a homecoming for us all because there is a home."[1] This longing is initiated not by us but by the grieving Father who is also our Creator. The divine invitation to "Come home!" is incredibly good news for *everyone*, offering the promise of forgiveness and great joy to both the prodigals and the dutiful pious. It is ours if we open ourselves and respond to the invitation because just as the prodigal did not earn forgiveness neither do the dutiful. It is ours by grace alone. The waiting Father longs for our company, not just our hard labor in the field.

1. Thielicke, *Waiting Father*, 29.

THE HERO CHILD

Like the self-righteous Pharisees monitoring Jesus, in the Gospel story the older son is pictured having no sense of wrongdoing in rejecting his brother or ignoring his father's plea to come to the party. Nevertheless, believing he is expected to do everything to keep the family farm afloat—to be the good, reliable one—is a heavy burden. He may not acknowledge it, but perhaps this is what is making him so disagreeable and rude to his father!

In pastoral situations I have seen many with an excessive sense of responsibility carry such a burden. One, a pastor struggling with burnout, told me how helpful it was to find his condition had a label and an explanation for his resentment and his desire to just let everything go. He identified himself as a Hero Child who was carrying too heavy a load of expectation—an expectation that he always be totally capable and good. And always responsible for everyone. This false self-image had distorted not only his personal life but his ministry as well, and he longed to be rid of it.

I, too, have felt this anxiety—along with many others I presume—arising from my own and others' high aspirations for me. We fear we will never be enough. "Hero Child" usually has its origins in the family of origin, especially from being *the* responsible child. The very label makes me shudder. It reminds me of what was asked of me when I was too young—oldest child, always trying to please my parents, stepping in for my mother when she insisted on handing roles over to me—a young woman then whose gifts and inclinations did not fit easily into my community's dictates, yet having impossibly high aspirations for myself, as did others. I carried into adulthood this pressure of trying to please, and I see it in many other highly functioning adults and leaders. We have never done enough, never done it *well* enough, so we feel inadequate and afraid. We cannot let go of our desire for perfect performance and are ashamed of failing. And we resent the expectations placed on us.

Moreover, in the latter stages of life when so many things the Hero Child has achieved are dropping away, fear and shame may lead to the emotion of worthlessness many experience in retirement.

TRYING TO BE PERFECT

When I was young, I had not heard the expression "Hero Child" but kept noticing biblical commands to be perfect (for example, Matt 5:48). It gave rise to this same burden of expectation. I was afraid I was inadequate because I could never meet God's absolute standard. Even within the incredible relationship with the Good Father I was discovering, I was afraid I would slip and become an outsider to his wonderful divine intimacy. Fortunately, the fear made me delve into the meaning behind this biblical instruction. I found the same word for *to make complete, perfect* was used of the first disciples mending their nets and, just as a doctor sets a broken arm to make it perfect and usable again, so the fishermen mending their nets were returning them to how they were meant to be. Fortunately, restoring us to "how we are meant to be" is the Holy Spirit's responsibility, not ours. What a relief for a perfectionist, a Hero Child!

We Hero Children are unlikely to have the residue of straying in a prodigal way, nor the accumulation of severe hurts or trauma described in chapter 3, but we do need to be restored to a sense of wholeness. We will never achieve being perfect or free in ourselves, so we must hear again and again there is no slavery, no fear, no shame in the family of Jesus. We can learn to trust God's wisdom and his gradual renovation of our lives.

Moreover, if we accept the invitation to come in to the party, the Spirit can not only take away fear of failing, he can also remove old habits of self-criticism or lingering feelings of inadequacy. Our life (and work and family and ministry) may not be perfect, but that is less important than knowing that the Father's love is perfect. Said the apostle John towards the end of his long life, "There is no fear in love. But perfect love drives out fear, because fear has to do with punishment. The one who fears is not made perfect in love" (1 John 4:18).

COME JOIN THE PARTY

Jesus ended his story with a party. That should resonate as an expression of grace for dutiful and pious older brothers and sisters. If we accept the Father's invitation to come home, we can experience a great release, parallel to the relief the prodigal experienced in having a roof over his head, good food in his stomach, and the forgiveness from his father. For hardworking, dutiful people released from a lifetime of trying to be good, from the burden of unmet expectations, from depending on others' adulation to give them worth, what better way to celebrate than with a party!

Of course, parties cost money and take time away from what task-driven people think are more important things. To earnest older sons and daughters, celebrating may seem trivial and unnecessary in the grand scheme of things. But all of us are called to live by faith, not works. Celebration is a common way the Scriptures prompt us to respond to God with thanksgiving and delight.

In the early days of their nation, at God's direction Moses instructed the Hebrews how to live with gratitude and grace by prescribing many festivals and feasts. These were more than a catchy dance to a fiddler on the roof. They included important symbols and actions that taught and established traditions, and Jesus continued to celebrate them with his fellow Jewish disciples during his earthly years. Some he infused with even deeper meaning centered on his life's mission as the long-expected Messiah. Some, such as the Passover celebrating the exodus from Egyptian slavery, were fulfilled when he inaugurated his new covenant and became the setting for introducing the Christian celebration of Communion or the Eucharist, with its emphasis now for Jewish and gentile Christians alike on giving thanks for his saving death on the Roman cross. We celebrate the Lord's Supper with solemnity because of what the cross cost God in Jesus, but we should also be laughing with relief because it lifts the burden of our sin and inadequacy!

BABETTE'S FEAST

Feasts in the form of parties are pointers in Scripture to our standing in the presence of God on the basis of grace, not works of our own doing. The greatest of these is the wedding banquet at the end of time, but each feast before then has a background story presenting a great reason to celebrate. This is why the more recent narrative of Babette's Feast, first told by Isak Dinesen but also recounted by several other writers, is an equivalent contemporary story. It illustrates so well the triumph of generous grace over harsh religious piety—a piety which struggles to be warm and sustaining.[2]

The story tells of Babette, once a chef in faraway Paris, gratefully finding a home in her flight from persecution with two dour sisters in Denmark. These women are members of a severe Christian sect whose founder instructed them before his death to live seriously and frugally. Their whole community has obeyed him to an extreme.

2. Other writers include Smedes, *Shame and Grace*, and Keller, *Prodigal God*. The story has also been made into a movie, fittingly filmed in subdued black and white.

When Babette comes unexpectedly into a large sum of money, she decides to spend it on providing a lavish feast for this austere group of unsmiling people. Multiple boats with supplies arrive at the Danish town providing more food and elegant table settings than they have ever seen. Over the course of the meal, the men and women eat, drink, and gradually relax, acknowledging each other with new warmth as the Babette's generosity wears away their rigid solemnity. They have not shared such smiles and laughter for many years and so find a new understanding of their standing in amazing grace before their God.

HEAVEN IS A BANQUET

Feasting, even simple fellowship around a shared table, also gives us another way to emphasize the communal nature of our faith. Taking food in isolation may offer bodily sustenance, but it does not have the same value as connecting with people over food and drink. Words for taking large quantities of food such as *gorging yourself*, *binging*, or *indulging a sweet tooth* all suggest a scene of stressful and lonely isolation. Dieting, too, even when necessary for health reasons, does not have the sense of community a feast or banquet has.

During 2022 we were in England during the honoring of Queen Elizabeth II's platinum jubilee of coming to the throne. While visiting relatives, we were invited to join several "long tables" in local villages to be part of the celebrations. One of those local tables was in the town of a relative deeply grieving the recent death of his wife. To that point he had isolated himself, not wanting to face the sympathetic inquiries of his neighbors. Perhaps because his Australian relatives were there, he finally agreed to come down to the long table meal with us, and we saw the healing for him in meeting up again and chatting with friends and connections in his village.

A wedding banquet is also a great connecting occasion and in the book of Revelation is the picture of our ultimate union with God and all fellow believers. Jesus Christ the groom is its central focus, but there is also a beautiful bride—the believers, the church, us—whose "dowry" is paid with Jesus' sacrifice. Community, love, joy, family, and friendship are the themes, as food, music, and dancing all contribute symbolically to the celebration of coming together at the end of the age when the Creator is bringing heaven and earth together. No time for tears (or resentment); no dour duty at this table. The invitation to the wedding banquet from the Spirit and the bride says, "Come!" (Rev 22:17).

In a collection of sermons by Eugene Peterson, he describes this celebration of grace at the end of time as a "Hallelujah Banquet,"[3] noting that only in the book of Revelation does the New Testament use the Hebrew *hallelujah* shout of praise, and that, amazingly, by Christians suffering under severe persecution.

We do not need to wait till the last days or when we are living in comfort to express our gratitude and joy to God. We can do it now. Amen! Praise God! Hallelujah! "Blessed are those who are invited to the wedding supper of the Lamb!" (Rev 19:9). As the father in the Jesus' story says to *both* the prodigal *and* the grumpy older son, "Come! Come home! Come to the party!"

RELATIONSHIPS MATTER

The reluctance of task-oriented older sons and daughters to celebrate may point to a deeper problem, however. It is not just that they do not enjoy parties. They do not value relationships enough. Certainly, they are not willing to waste time just "chewing the cud" with others nor accepting the casual invitation to sit down to chat over a cup of tea or coffee.

I was mentally rebuked on a recent occasion when someone we knew came to our house. Almost as soon as he entered, my husband and I, both busy, dutiful people, immediately inquired about his purpose in coming to see us unexpectedly that day. No tea or coffee offered! Our guest was originally from Africa, and in that moment I was sharply reminded by my conscience that in any one of the African societies where I have been welcomed, a visit would begin with a handshake all round, an offer of a glass of water or cup of tea, and an extended time of personal connection followed by inquiries about one's health and family. Open rapport would be established before any business was entered into.

I was also reminded of a cultural puzzle. Many years ago, when I first began visiting in East African countries, in addition to the handshakes and conversation, the welcome often included deliberately turning the TV *on*. It seemed like a contradiction of the emphasis on personal connection that I experienced there. In Australia we do the opposite if someone drops into our house unexpectedly. We turn the TV *off*! My speculation is that in the not-so-distant past, not all homes in that part of Africa had TV, so viewing

3. Peterson, *This Hallelujah Banquet*.

it was an extra luxury offered as a gift to the guest. Generous hospitality indeed.

In contrast, an Asian friend once told us that he pitied Westerners—we were too driven by our clock watching, by our desire for efficiency. "What would Jesus do?" he continued in rebuke. "He stopped and talked to whoever came across his path—because valuing the person was far more important than any time constraints or immediate agenda." Divergent attitudes to time can simply be part of cultural differences, just as the way we dress or eat, yet there is truth in his criticism. We are poorer when we neglect opportunities for connecting and valuing the people around us.

CHOOSING RELATIONSHIP

There are different levels of relating, starting simply with *connection*. Over the back fence, in the lunchroom, before a committee meeting, or with a cup of coffee in hand, if for no other reason, it is good for our social and mental health to know and be known by others. Connecting lays the groundwork for a more significant relationship and belonging. It may be superficial and hardly enough, yet it is nevertheless important for what it offers in the present moment as well as where it can lead in the future. Time given as a gift is not wasted!

Telling our stories is a good way to begin mutual sharing, the next level of relating. It gradually reveals to each other our histories, values, and everyday patterns of life. It may develop out of finding we share something in common, but in the longer term we are made richer by our complementary differences as we bring varying backgrounds and perspectives to offer to each other in a wider understanding of humanity and our world.

The deepest level of relating is *heart-to-heart*, walking life together. We do this in marriage and family and with long-term friends. But it can also be a chosen practice for a more limited and intentional time by engaging with a mentor or joining a small group. All such relationships have the potential to grow empathy in us, overcoming the "I'm better than you" posture that leads to the kind of isolation the older son represents. His standoff attitude, like the pious purity and fear of contamination practiced by the Pharisees, separates us from our fellow human beings in a way never intended. God created us for relationship, mirroring the three-in-one image of the Godhead in which we were created.

When our brothers and sisters in Christ offer us this deep intimacy, it need not compete with our biological family to whom we also owe time and energy. But using New Testament language, we are encouraged to relate to our church communities as a family, the family of God. Deep relationships make demands on us, of course, so they must be given more than an hour on a Sunday. But it is good value for us and the other for the time and emotional energy invested and particularly important on the personal level for "older brothers and sisters."

We also know that any schism in a human family brings enormous and possibly long-lasting sorrow. Similarly, misunderstandings and divisions in a church family bring pain to our Father and deprive us of the friendship and support of brothers and sisters if we let them or fail to repent of them. The self-righteous older son is no model in his rectitude or disconnection. He needs his family and the welcome home just as much as his younger brother, and so do we.

A LONELY SOCIETY

We Westerners live in lonely societies. Our culture does not place enough importance on the committed human relationships that promote flourishing. The figures for social isolation are staggering and represent a serious health risk, especially for the growing proportion of older people who are segregated in their houses. For example, a recently released Australian State of the Nation Report into social connection, entitled *Ending Loneliness Together* (2023), reported on a survey of four thousand adult Australians. Nearly one-third said they felt lonely or disconnected often. Surprisingly however, the peak level of loneliness reported was in the eighteen to twenty-four years of age group (22 percent), where it was associated with a high degree of social media addiction.[4] The report described loneliness as debilitating, as debilitating as physical food hunger. Moreover, people who reported frequent loneliness were found to be many times more likely to suffer from chronic disease, depression, social anxiety, and overall poorer wellbeing.[5]

Social psychologist Hugh Mackay, a longtime observer of Western society, has written extensively about this social trend. In his recent book *The Way We Are*, he heads the opening section, "The Context: Born to Connect

4. Ending Loneliness Together, *State of the Nation Report*, 13, 34.
5. Ending Loneliness Together, *State of the Nation Report*, 22–25.

but Lonelier than Ever" and reports statistics similar to the survey mentioned above. He lists several observable factors in current society likely contributing to this social isolation and loneliness. These include shrinking family size, breakdown of marriage, increasing numbers of children living with only one parent, less neighborhood connection due to house design and block size, frequent changes of address, general busyness, and greater use of social media and working from home in place of face-to-face connection.[6] These are not just Australian trends but worldwide.

But he also names the decline in religious life and practices as a factor because people are focusing more on themselves and less on mixing with and serving others. Mackay does not claim to write from a Christian perspective, but he frequently uses terms such as "born to connect" and "social hunger" and describes humans as a "social species." He says, "Beware of busyness: it's the enemy of social cohesion. And therefore, for members of a social species, it's the enemy of mental health too."[7]

This is a challenge for those of us inclined to be older sons and daughters, feeling secure and vindicated in our self-righteousness. The tendency to individualism in contemporary values we discussed in chapter 6 and here requires countering because it is not God's intention nor good for any of us.

We will return in a later chapter to explore how modeling good relationships as Christians is part of our family heritage and a benefit we can offer to our society as heirs in the family of God. But first, beyond enjoying a good party, there is another aspect of our generous inheritance pictured in Scripture. It is the privilege of being adopted by the God of the universe and of sharing our family with Jesus, the royal Son. That is what we must explore next.

RESPONDING

- If you are the grumpy older son rather than the prodigal coming home, how do you react to that label? Do you resent being compared to a Pharisee?
- Has being a conscientious, duty-oriented person given an austere tinge to your life? Does a party seem an appropriate way to celebrate

6. Mackay, *Way We Are*, 7–49.

7. Mackay, *Way We Are*, 25.

the freedom you have now found in the Good Father? If not, how else can you celebrate?

- You may have some lonely people living around you. What small changes can you make to connect with them and build community?
- Perhaps you find yourself lonely. Ponder what you can do to respond to that realization and so connect more deeply with your Christian brothers and sisters, family, or community.

8

Now We Are Heirs

If I find in myself a desire which no experience in this world can satisfy, the most probable explanation is that I was made for another world. . . . Probably earthly pleasures were never meant to satisfy it, but only to arouse it, to suggest the real thing.

—C. S. Lewis, *Mere Christianity*

Novelist Walker Percy tells a story about people marooned on an island.[1] They were descendants of castaways from shipwrecks on its coast but had forgotten their origins and lived happily on their island paradise where they developed a community in which all their needs were met. One day, one of the islanders walking on the beach found a bottle washed up on the sand. Inside a note said simply, "Help is coming." This islander had everything he desired and was not aware there was an outside world, so the message did not make sense, and he discarded it. A few weeks later, however, he found another bottle, and this time the note said, "Help will arrive soon, don't give up." Still, it did not make sense. He did not think he needed any help, and where would it come from anyway. He was not aware of any other world than his.

But the man told a friend, and together they looked for other bottles, finding one from time to time. Each had a similar message. "Help left

1. Percy, *Message in the Bottle.*

yesterday." Or "Take heart, help will certainly come." The word got out, and others joined in the search. The strange words stirred something deep in them, some memory of another world, some suggestion that all they had was *not* all. Of course, there were scoffers who refused to join the search and thought it was ridiculous. They had everything they required to explain the world as they experienced it. Yet these words from someone outside which they did not understand had a curious draw on them. It sounded as if it was a life and death matter, that without this help they were lost. They wanted to know more about it. From time to time, they would get together and read the fragmentary messages. They still did not understand them, but it was important to know these were messages from elsewhere, perhaps from a mainland to which this island belonged.

THE UNSEEN SPIRITUAL WORLD

Many people are like these island residents, unaware of spiritual realities until they come upon a message that there is something greater available from outside their self-contained world. We Westerners, in particular, have grown up with a worldview that tells us that only what can be seen and touched is real. The nonconcrete spiritual world is suspect. Or dangerous.

It may be the birth of our first child that almost overwhelms us and sends us a message. Touched by a love that is beyond anything they have previously experienced, even brusque new fathers dare to talk about it with their friends. Or grief at the death of a loved one may be a message in a bottle pointing to some greater meaning as we become aware of a spiritual dimension of life more intense and sudden than we expected or can control.

On the other hand, as we noted in chapter 6, many people in Western society now search for the missing fullness of life and identity in expressive individualism, thinking reality is found only in the *self*. But when that *self* is not enough, they become aware of a bigger world beyond their island.

One of my former colleagues had a weeknight radio talk-back broadcast in Perth. Though it was not a religious program, time and time again people rang in to ask Graham to pray for them about a health issue or a wayward child or a marriage disintegrating. Perhaps until that point in their lives they had not thought they needed any outside help, but now they were fervently hoping there was an unseen spiritual power, and they wanted to tap into it through their *Nightline* host who they knew was also a pastor. They had, as it were, picked up a bottle that had a message of "Help is available" but did not know where to find the mainland of spiritual reality except through him.

MORE THAN VAGUE SPIRITUALITY

Spirituality is a useful word that has been used for the search for this greater reality, but its use has become vague, largely inward-looking, and often unconnected to God who is Spirit. When we prodigals (or older sons and daughters) have come home to the Father, we are saying in effect, "I have tried to run my own life, but now I recognize there is a greater reality. All I can see and touch and manage myself in my ordinary desires or routines is not enough. Good Father, I need more of you in my life. I accept with open hands the fullness of true life you want to give me in the divine realm."

With this receptive attitude, we are acknowledging a spiritual dimension of life, but we often stop there. We do not realize it involves all that we are—body and emotions and psyche in a mainland we can explore for the rest of our lives—a reality that encompasses everything and goes beyond anything we have known to date. This is what distinguishes us from animals and machines. We are created to be like God, more like the Creator than anything else he has made. And we relate to him and one another as spiritual beings—people with bodies and minds and personalities—but people made to live now and forever in the unseen world as well as in the seen. We have access to a power in all areas of our lives so that what is in the spiritual realm becomes visible in our everyday lives. Like the wind we cannot see but know its presence by its effect; so the spiritual wind can be seen in our lived experience.

However, not all in the spiritual realm is good or intends good towards us. The immaterial world contains forces we label demons, personifying them. It also includes structures or practices of society that, even if intended to benefit a community or a culture, work towards its dislocation or destruction. We are often oblivious to these powers, these invisible "rulers and authorities in the heavenly realms" as the apostle Paul calls them (Eph 3:10). Then we come up against them in our personal or work lives as we are seeking to bring change for good, or when we cannot explain widespread societal attitudes that stand in the way of that positive good. But once alerted, we gain a deeper understanding of the invisible spiritual world and of the power now and in the future of the risen and ascended Christ to overcome evil forces.[2]

SPIRITUALITY THROUGH THE HOLY SPIRIT

First, however, we must note that the biblical term for the good power operating in this unseen reality is a person, not an impersonal force. He is the third person of the Godhead: God the Holy Spirit. And *holy* Spirit, not just any spirit, because as we have seen previously *holy* means, among other things, that God can be trusted. He has no part in evil. This must be said because although most people familiar with Christian teaching know of the Holy Spirit, his work is often ignored or misunderstood or thought of acting like a magic wand. Ignored by Western-raised people skeptical about the unseen world; or in contrast, ignored when hunger for mystical experience sends them off into other forms of spirituality, despite this great gift of the indwelling Holy Spirit we have been offered.

It is through the Holy Spirit that we experience the love and acceptance of the Good Father whose generosity and forgiveness we have been celebrating. Jesus whetted our appetite for this with his story of the son coming home to the waiting father and the older son urged to join the party. As we have seen, prodigals creeping home for a meal and a roof over their heads get much more than that. They are offered intimacy with the Good Father, forgiveness, and the healing of their hurts and scars and shame. And older sons coming in, recognizing their need for the family relationship, receive relief from the burden of self-effort and bitterness. What both prodigals and older sons experience in the Father's house is mediated through the Holy Spirit.

ADOPTED INTO GOD'S FAMILY

To appreciate the possibilities available in this spiritual dimension, we need another story, another metaphor, to enter into the wonders of ongoing transformation. When the apostle Paul writes to the first-century churches in Galatia and Rome about these riches available to Christians, he uses, as did Jesus, a picture of a father; this time instead of welcoming a prodigal

2. More on this topic is found in Wink, *Powers That Be*, and Wright and Bird, *Jesus and the Powers*.

home, it is a father *adopting* a new son into his family. C. S. Lewis said of this biblical idea of adoption, "When the Bible talks of our 'becoming' Sons of God . . . that brings us up against the very centre of Theology."[3]

Paul's readers would have been familiar with the Greco-Roman practice of a father who, not having a satisfactory son and heir, adopts a lower-born adult or near adult male and treats him like a fully privileged biological son. The benefits would be gratefully and obediently received by the adopted son, but the initiative and the providing are all the father's.

Adoption today is not always seen as a positive practice in Western society, with heartrending stories told of people searching in adulthood for their birth mother (or father) even when they have been raised lovingly by another family. Certainly, we need to acknowledge the harm caused by forced adoptions in the past, when many young unwed mothers were pressured to surrender their child at birth because they were told they would not be able to give their offspring a good life. The very natural desire of a mother to care for the child of her own body was discounted. We also rightly have reservations now about raising Indigenous children in families, even devoted ones, without knowledge of their heritage. Much harm was done to Australian Indigenous "stolen generations" when that policy was used to try to eliminate a whole culture.

However, in the Greco-Roman culture of Paul's day, patrician families adopting a male and treating him as their own son with inheritance rights was thought a great benefit, offering a path out of poverty to the boy or man and opening access for him to education and an elevated standing in society. The adopting father initiated the relationship, but it came with the expectation that the adopted son would willingly come under his authority because he had so much to gain from the privilege.

Using this picture, Paul reminds us of the wonderful heritage we have as God's sons (and daughters).[4]

> Because you are his sons, God sent the Spirit of his Son into our hearts, the Spirit who calls out, "*Abba*, Father." So you are no longer a slave, but God's child; and since you are his child, God has made you also an heir. (Gal 4:6–7)

3. Lewis, *Mere Christianity*, 157.

4. The new covenant that Jesus inaugurated includes daughters (Gal 3:28). But because the Greco-Roman practice included only males, and Paul parallels it with the divine Sonship of Jesus who in his humanity was male, when "and daughters" is added in this chapter it is placed in parentheses.

PRIVILEGED ACCESS

The apostle has two central messages in this adoption metaphor. The first is to remind us of the privileged access, the incredible intimacy, we have with the adopting Father. He borrows into his Greek narrative the Aramaic family name for father, *Abba*, to emphasize the great privilege of being invited to come close to the high holy God, close enough and intimately enough to call God *Abba! Father!*

Jesus used this family word as he prayed to his Father in Gethsemane, no doubt contemplating the pain and separation he faced going to the cross. About to be handed over to his killers and agonizing over what lay ahead of him, he prays, "Abba, Father, everything is possible for you. Take this cup from me" (Mark 14:36). This cry brings to mind a child desperately calling out, knowing their father will hear them despite all the surrounding noise and turmoil. Then Jesus adds, "Yet not what I will, but what you will." *Abba* also implies revering the father and submitting to him.

What a comfort it must have been in Gethsemane for Jesus to cry out in anguish to the Father! As God's heirs we have the same privilege of speaking to God in similar familiar terms, praying, "Abba!" (Gal 4:4–7, Rom 8:14–17).

The Message Bible paraphrase renders *Abba!* as *Papa!* just as we might say *Dad* when addressing our father within the family, though we might refer to him as *father* outside it. Some Christians, wanting to savor this closeness, use *Daddy* or *Papa* when they pray. I understand the sense of privileged intimacy these words represent, but I cannot myself switch to calling God *Daddy* or *Papa*. Although *Papa* was the familiar name my paternal grandfather took, I never knew that grandfather and did not use it as a family term when I was a child. Moreover, while *Abba* is indeed the cry of a child to their father, my now-adult sons no longer call their father *Daddy*. *Dad* seems more appropriate for grown men to use, while *Father* would be too formal in the Australian cultural landscape. But whichever term we use in prayer to our Good Father, we can appreciate, luxuriate in, the wonder and confidence of being invited into the presence of the God of creation, the God of the universe, whom Jesus addressed as *Abba*.

That this treasured family relationship is offered to us cannot be stated too strongly or too often! The Godhead family invites us into its very center to be surrounded by its love. It is not easy to grasp the Father-Son-Spirit relationship, but we can think of it as a divine circle dance without beginning or end—a dance of equals, giving and receiving, in perfect unison. It has the idea of indwelling, of oneness, because the participants in this Godhead dance are not separate entities but one God.[5] And we are invited into the midst of that! Privilege indeed! But no excuse at all for hubris, pride, or self-sufficiency.

Yet how easily we forget this privilege. We drift back to trying to run our lives without reference to the One who has opened his home to us. Or on the other hand, we sometimes presume that whatever we ask for will be given to us, like putting coins in a vending machine and seeing the food or drink we have ordered drop to the open hatch at the bottom. Or over time, we give the relationship with this loving Father less and less space in our busy schedules. We need Holy Spirit reminders of what is ours as God's children and what a privilege it is. Jesus told his disciples that just as the Father had sent him in the world, so he was sending his Spirit into our hearts because it is the Spirit's role to keep prompting us to enjoy the intimacy of access we have received (John 14:16–21).

Paul adds, "Don't grieve God. Don't break his heart. His Holy Spirit, moving and breathing in you, is the most intimate part of your life, making you fit for himself. Don't take such a gift for granted" (Eph 4:30 MSG).

WHO IS ADOPTED?

Paul uses this picture of being adopted in the same way Jesus used parables, emphasizing one main aspect to make the point, and sometimes modifying the details of the historic practice in surprising ways for use in his illustration. By his saying we are *adopted* by God, first to the Galatian Christians and then to the Romans (8:14–17), Paul highlights their new freedom to relate to God as children to a father, to converse with him as Jesus did, to have complete access to him with incredible intimacy. Though they owe their new family head respect and obedience, they are no longer slaves.

The surprising thing in Paul's use of this cultural picture for our relationship with God is that the privilege is open to all, not just to males, as in Greco-Roman culture. It is for all who come home to God the Father. He tells the Galatian Christians that through the cross of Jesus' sacrifice, not just Hebrews but all believers are considered descendants of Abraham and inherit the Abrahamic promises. There are no ethnic, status, or gender

5. Commentators such as Jürgen Moltmann, Miroslav Volf, and Richard Rohr have found this circle dance a useful way to explore the theology of the Trinity.

boundaries. All descendants—of whatever ethnicity, slaves as well as free, women as well as men—are adopted "children of God through faith" and enter into this special relationship with God the Father (Gal 3:26–28). No need to strive for respectability or acceptance, the Good Father initiates the adoption and bestows it freely, warmly calling us his sons (and daughters). And as we noted previously, the early church picked up this inclusive language and delighted in calling each other brothers and sisters in God's family.

Some consider all people are God's children, and in one sense we are because God created us. But the Scriptures reserve the right to become "children of God" for those who receive Jesus, who believe in his name (John 1:12–13). Our standing as son or daughter, brother or sister, is secured by our accepting adoption. It is God-initiated, but we have the right to turn down the offer. But if we accept, "God's Spirit touches our spirits and confirms who we really are: Father and children. And we know we are going to get what's coming to us—an unbelievable inheritance!" (Rom 8:16–17a MSG).

LIVING THE RELATIONSHIP

The prodigal son coming back home would have understood how unexpected it was to be receiving the privilege of full inclusion in the family again. Jesus says in the story that as he left the pigsty and headed back, the young man thought that all he could expect was to be treated as a servant on his return. Instead, the father warmly accepts him as a son. He has been looking out for him, waiting for him, wanting him back, and throws his arms around him once again in welcome. The older brother would also experience the father's warm embrace if he let himself be enfolded into the family.

In Australia today with its high cost of property and shortage of houses, the thing most children probably think they want to inherit is the family home, hoping not to have to wait till the parents die to get it! This is not surprising. A physical home is such an essential thing! A safe roof over your head makes possible many of life's essential tasks and responsibilities. Secure living arrangements help you get a job, enable you to care for a family, and allow you to share hospitality with others as you build friendships. But it is only the beginning. A house is not a home!

In a similar way, coming home to God and the unconditional acceptance he offers his children, both prodigal and older brother, is only the beginning of a new life for Christians who have put their faith and future in him. We believers, we adopted sons (and daughters), have the opportunity to realize all the benefits that are ours as heirs.

One writer bemoaned that many Christians neglect the glorious heritage they have as Christ's bride (the church), calling his book *Cinderella with Amnesia*.[6] The Cinderella bride has forgotten all that is hers since she was rescued by the prince. We sons (and daughters) can also have amnesia, forgetting all we have since we were welcomed home and adopted by our Good Father.

HEIRS GROW IN THE FATHER'S LOVE

As we saw earlier, a starting point for enjoying an incredible intimacy with God is simply asking for what we need, in prayer. Help is available, even in the asking. When we do not know what to pray for, the Holy Spirit asks on our behalf (Rom 8:26–27). Of course, such asking would be presumptuous if we had not been invited into this wonderful relationship with the Father, or if we used our connection only to lodge a weekly shopping list. We also know that prayer is more than asking, just as a good relationship between partners in marriage, or children with a parent, is more than asking. It includes enjoying the companionship, coming to know the *other* ever more deeply, and loving them more and more as the years roll on.

So it is with our continuing connection with God. From his side, he cannot love us more or want us to be with him more than when we first came home to his welcoming arms. But *we* can grow in our appreciation and response to him, learning how to balance that growing familiarity with due respect and reverence for the high and holy One, and without fear. When we falter in making space for this incredible intimacy in our frantic lives, we need to stop and remember *who* it is who invites us into his presence. To grow in knowing God is the unearned privilege we have as adopted sons (and daughters) through Jesus.

Nevertheless, we will not always experience the prodigal's high excitement coming home to love and forgiveness; or as an older brother, grasping the relief of being *enough*, no longer having to rely for acceptance on compliance or competence.

In marriage, we soon realize after the wedding that we cannot spend day-to-day life in the ecstasy of first love. We cannot honeymoon totally and forever, expecting a continuous elevated sensual level! It would make

6. Griffiths, *Cinderella with Amnesia.*

ordinary activities such as working, cooking, and cleaning impossible! There are certain life essentials that just need to be done. But we also know that time together as a couple or family, expressing appreciation and serving one another, is essential to sustaining and growing the relationship.

DAILY WITH THE GOOD FATHER

Sometimes people tell me that in the past they used to *hear* God speak to them or *felt* his presence tangibly, but now spending regular time with him feels dry, almost a duty. In this situation, Thielicke reminds us to focus on the privilege we have, not the feeling:

> It is quite enough if every day the first thing we do in our morning prayer is to give thanks that we are even *permitted* to speak with God, that he has promised to listen to us, and that we may lay all the burdens of our heart before him.[7]

C. S. Lewis puts it in his characteristic way:

> All your wishes and hopes for the day rush at you like wild animals. And the first job each morning consists simply in shoving them all back; in listening to that other voice, taking that other point of view, letting that other, larger, stronger, quieter life come flowing in.[8]

Some mornings (if that is the time we have reserved for meeting with our Good Father), we receive no dramatic revelations in prayer or from the Scriptures, but day by day God is building our understanding of him and his ways and making deposits in us of spiritual insights that can be called on later. My personal response to dryness in my relationship with my heavenly Father is to remember that relating also includes times of just doing things together, serving him using the gifts and resources he has given me.

Important, too, is discovering how personally we best respond to this divine relationship. Here the concept of love languages may be useful.[9] We are each different in what reminds us how greatly we are loved by God. For me, it is words of affirmation, and I hear them through reading the psalms, which capture the full range of human emotions from praise, gratitude, anger, frustration, love, desire, and acceptance to resilience.

7. Thielicke, *Waiting Father*, 34.
8. Lewis, *Mere Christianity*, 169.
9. Terminology applied to personal relationships by Chapman, *Five Love Languages*.

They provide me with a language to hear God speak and to explore my response to *Abba* Father.

We can build other routines into daily life to foster intimacy with God by experimenting with what works for us in our current season of life. This might include finding a sustainable way and time to read the Scriptures, regularly enjoying biographies of God-followers, immersing oneself in songs or poetry associated with Scriptures that have come to mind, and sharing with a friend or mentor. Journal entries, voice recordings, or computer notes can capture the insights received and later provide the discernment we need.

HOPE NOW AND FOR THE FUTURE

Romans 8 is a chapter which we often turn to for comfort in a demanding everyday life. Yet Paul acknowledges that in the present time we children of God are still waiting for the full implications in our bodies of our sonship. Our adoption inheritance is not fully realized until we are resurrected into God's presence on the other side of death. We live in the "now but not yet," but this need not discourage us. As one Bible commentator explains,

> The inheritance has to do with eternal confidence in the Father's covenant and providing love. Paul comes back . . . to the Father who has given us himself in his Son and therefore can be trusted to give us everything else as well (v. 32). This present and providing love may be utterly trusted in the midst of accusation and condemnation, all physical deprivation, religious persecution, demonic interference, natural calamity (vv. 34–39).[10]

This is present reality, encouraging us as we go on living in a damaged and damaging world. Much of our inheritance through our relationship with God is available here and now. In other words, we inherit from our Father much more than "going home" to heaven at the end of our physical life. We will explore in chapter 11 what that popular expression means for a Christian.

There is, however, a second central message in this adoption metaphor, a further gem of life-affirming truth in Paul calling us God's sons (and daughters) by adoption. He includes the astounding statement that we are coheirs with Jesus Christ (Rom 8:17). Jesus, too, is a son—Son from

10. Smail, *Forgotten Father*, 158.

before the beginning, the "Word" at creation, as the apostle John tells us (John 1:1–4). Translators into English make clear Jesus' elevated standing by giving *Son* a capital letter.

This sonship with Jesus the Son will be explored in the next chapter when we focus specifically on Jesus. For not only is Jesus our model for relating to the Good Father, it is his sacrifice for sin that makes possible our full and free forgiveness in God's presence.

RESPONDING

- Meditate on Galatians 4:6–7. Young children take for granted the love and security their parents provide. Even if such care is not their daily experience, they still expect to receive it. Later in life if they have not had family love and security, it can cause great anger and disappointment. Is that your experience? As God's child, you can be confident of *this Father's* love and acceptance and healing of any hurts and scars you bring to the Good Father. Welcome the Holy Spirit to remind you of this as often as necessary.
- *The Message* paraphrase renders Romans 8:15, "This resurrection life you received from God is not a timid, grave-tending life. It's adventurously expectant, greeting God with a childlike 'What's next, Papa?'" Is that how you are facing life?
- Do you feel pressure to be perfect? Or feel shame when you interrogate yourself? As a prompt for living every moment in God's loving presence, it may be helpful to begin the day with "Good morning, Father!" and end it at night with a "Thank you, Father!"

9

Jesus Is in the House

I remain convinced that the very heartbeat of the universe is love, and his name is Jesus.

—STEVE CUSS, *THE EXPECTATION GAP*

In an early chapter of the Gospel of Mark there is a revealing story about Jesus. He has come home to Capernaum, the town where he grew up, and many people, having heard of his growing reputation as a healer, overflow the house and spill outside, expecting more demonstrations of his healing power. Instead, when a paralyzed man is lowered to him through the roof by some enterprising friends, Jesus says to the man, "Son, your sins are forgiven" (Mark 2:5). This is heard as blasphemy, especially by the religious guardians present. "Who can forgive sins but God alone?" they mutter to themselves (verse 7). In response, Jesus affirms that not only healing but forgiving is within his power because he is indeed God. In Jesus, God entered our world as a human being—the Son, one in the Godhead with the Father and the Holy Spirit. In fact, through the Son's relationship with the one he taught us to call Father, we get an expanding understanding of that three-in-one Godhead, of God.

We struggle to grasp all that it means that the man Jesus is God. We read accounts of his life in the four Gospels and see his actions and stories illustrating the best of being human. But here in his hometown he is challenging the idea, still common today, that he was just a compassionate, godly man with a gift for healing and teaching. Jesus' startling words insist that a productive and fulfilling human life beyond physical healing is possible, but it starts with forgiveness.

THE ANSWER IS JESUS

There is a story about a child in Sunday school who discovered that when his teacher asked them a Bible question, if he said "Jesus," it was often the answer his teacher was looking for! There is some truth in this! The answer is Jesus so many times. And it applies here too.

We began this book with the story of a father who had two sons. And though our focus has been on God the Good Father, and then in the last chapter, on the third person of the Godhead, the Holy Spirit, we must now turn our spotlight on Jesus the divine Son, because through his humanity, his death, his resurrection, and now, following his ascension, his intervention of our behalf, all comes through him. Love lived out in Jesus' life is the heartbeat of the universe, Steve Cuss reminds us.

Timothy Keller used *prodigal* in the title of his book on this story[1] to describe the lavish, unexpected, recklessly extravagant love the father shows to both his sons. Thielicke, too, chooses to focus on *The Waiting Father*, the title of his sermon on the story, but both writers acknowledge that Jesus the Son is pivotal to the story. Thielicke adds,

> So Jesus, who tells this parable, is pointing to himself, between the lines and back of every word. . . . And he is not merely telling us about this Father; the Father himself is *in* him. . . . Is he not the very voice of the Father's heart that overtakes us in the far country and tells us that incredibly joyful news, "You can come home. Come home!"?[2]

We cannot luxuriate in the intimacy we have with the Father (chapter 2) without acknowledging that God the Son was one with the Father in calling us home. The healing of our hurts and scars through God's power and acceptance (chapter 3) is demonstrated in Jesus' dealings with ordinary people during his days of walking the dusty roads of Palestine. We hear him calling himself a shepherd and caring for us; we see him healing people with a confidence and readiness that others cannot match; and he

1. Keller, *Prodigal God.*
2. Thielicke, *Waiting Father*, 28–29.

tells us stories that we both love and puzzle over, just as he intended for people then, and subsequent generations, to do. But there are two more features of the person and work of Jesus the Son that help us understand the riches we have in being home with the Good Father.

The first, forgiveness, is illustrated by the Capernaum story which opens this chapter. Being forgiven is an enormous relief. The crippled man lowered through the roof of the house would have experienced that. We know it too, but we are also aware that an offense lightly excused without acknowledgement of its evil or hurt is not enough. Even when forgiveness is offered by a person of significance, a penalty must apply because forgiving has a cost—a cost played out in sacrifice, even the self-sacrifice of the one offended by the violation but who is choosing to forgive.

THE COST OF FORGIVENESS

The hearers of Jesus' story about the two sons would have been alert to the wrong done by the prodigal to his father and understood the depth of the forgiveness he offered by accepting him back into the family. At the very least, it cost the father his dignity to run to greet and forgive his son. And in his society, he risked public condemnation for being too lenient on him when he was expected to shun him. The father was also prepared to surrender any remaining respect his older son had for him by going out to plead with that son to come into the celebration.

For God in Jesus, the cost of forgiving us was Jesus' death on a cross. His resurrection to life again after three days signaled a new beginning for all of us who come home to this loving and forgiving God. Many of us, however, even some who identify as a prodigal, resent being called sinners needing forgiveness. We may be aware of how often we fall short, not just of God's standards but of our own values, but we excuse it thinking, "I'm no worse than anyone else!" or "What can you expect when we live in such an ugly/demanding/chaotic world?" Nevertheless, deep down we want to get rid of the continuing weight of our expectations and self-criticism. We hate our habit of repeated failure, failing again and again to live up to our values, despite our good intentions. And we know God's standard of godliness is even higher than our own.

So when we turn and come home to God's open arms, the forgiveness made possible through Jesus' death and rising is a gift to relish. It assures us we are acceptable to God, even though we know further renovation of our hearts is on the agenda. And any lingering self-doubt, any self-loathing, the Spirit starts to deal with now we are home, making us more and more like Jesus.

The Bible uses many metaphors to describe the paying of this cost—sacrifice for sin, reconciliation sealed in blood, a ransom given and accepted, a free pardon granted. Not one of these pictures of rescue is enough to fully encompass the wonder of judgment and justice satisfied, or of a clean conscience given to fallen people. "God was reconciling the world to himself in Christ, not counting people's sins against them," says the apostle Paul, summarizing the good news he has the privilege to share (2 Cor 5:19).

How amazing the sacrifice Jesus made! What humility for the Creator of the universe to accept human limitations and be born into our time and world! We can but stand in awe of the love expressed in Jesus' death and receive thankfully his gift of pardon.

COHEIRS WITH JESUS THE SON

The second feature of the God-man Jesus that is relevant here is his designation as *Son* of God. The capital letter for *Son* in English translations indicates an important distinction. As we saw in chapter 8, when we come home to the Father, we are adopted as his sons and daughters and have the privilege of an intimate relationship with *Abba, Father* through the Holy Spirit—the kind of access modeled by Jesus. But only Jesus is the perfect Son, the Son from eternity. "When the time arrived that had been set by God the Father, God sent his Son, born among us of a woman. . . . Thus we have been set free to experience our rightful heritage" (Gal 4:4–5 MSG). Through Jesus we receive our sonship and become coheirs with him, our very special brother, but our sonship is not from eternity like his, neither can we earn it. God the Father in his grace is adopting us—a difference Paul observes in the Rom 8 passage by using the word *children* for us, instead of *sons*.

Part of this *heritage* of being God's sons and daughters is that we are slaves no longer. We do not need to remain controlled by old habits and ways of thinking. One of these habits is trying to run our own life without reference to our Father. It is the most harmful attitude we can have (Rom 8:5). We slip so easily into thinking we know best how to live. We are like the woman and man in the garden at the beginning who doubted their Creator wanted only good for them and took things into their own hands.

Or like the prodigal son, having been accepted back into the household, if he had spurned his father and left again, still not caring how his actions affected his family. Or alternatively, like the older son continuing to see no need to come into the party because he considered he had done enough to earn the father's love, and that should satisfy him.

Trying to run our own life is the key word because we cannot actually do it. We could not do it before we came home and discovered God's forgiveness through Jesus, and we cannot do it now if we ignore the help of the Holy Spirit. In the first six chapters of his letter to the Romans, Paul describes the wonderful release from the slavery of sin available through Jesus' death and rising. But in the next chapter he finds it necessary to warn of the danger of reverting to old selfish ways of living, just like the prodigal might, or the older brother. He calls this being in slavery again, controlled by addictions, and illustrates it from his own experience: "For I have the desire to do what is good, but I cannot carry it out. For I do not do the good I want to do, but the evil I do not want to do—this I keep on doing" (Rom 7:18–19).

Each of us could quickly make a long list of things we have tried over the course of our life to leave behind: habits or attitudes or substances we know are not good but cannot easily shake off. We must remember that as God's adopted and loved children, we are no longer slaves to these. We must conduct ourselves as befitting our new status as sons and daughters of the Good Father. But how?

JESUS IS OUR MODEL FOR LIVING

Being adopted in the first century was not all lounging around and doing your own thing in your newly privileged position. The Greco-Roman father expected his sons to listen to him and follow his instructions, respecting and obeying him without question. In our relationship with the Good Father, we, too, must practice hearing God's voice and obeying. Some of how to do that we learn from examining Jesus' teaching recorded for us in Scripture, but, more poignantly, we learn it by examining Jesus' own obedience to the mission which directed his human life. He was the man for others. Asked what following God meant for disciples at the deepest level, Jesus summed it up as *love God, love others* (Matt 22:34–40). We, too, are to love and serve our Father and love and serve others as Jesus, our coheir, did.

In Jesus the Son we see the best of human qualities we long for: patience with awkward people and those who do not understand us or make insistent demands on us; compassion for those devalued or feared in the society—the women, the sick, the lepers, the troubled in mind, bumbling followers. We read how marginalized people felt safe with him and allowed him to touch them, even lovingly correct them. We are inspired by his prayer life, and his steadfastness in mission despite its cost, and by his teaching.

Most of all, we are encouraged by Jesus' example to live, as he did, in the power of God through the Holy Spirit, receiving spiritual insight, making choices, and understanding people in a way that does not diminish them but gives them power and insight too. We have in Jesus a mirror, showing us what we can become now we are heirs of the Father, *his* Father. These wonderful qualities can be summed up in Paul's listing of the fruit of a life lived in the Spirit: love, joy, peace, forbearance, kindness, goodness, faithfulness, gentleness, and self-control (Gal 5:22–23).

Does this sound like we can turn into perfect human beings? Though we have a wonderful model in this chief Son, and though we see in him the full potential of being human as the Creator intended, we cannot produce Jesus' qualities in our lives by our own effort. Acknowledging this is the essential starting point.

Dallas Willard, and later John Ortberg, point to parallels with the Alcoholics Anonymous approach to recovery which starts with accepting one's need and being open to a higher power's help. Step 1 in AA reads, "We admitted we were powerless over our deepest problems—that our lives had become unmanageable."[3] Step 2 follows with, "We came to believe that a Power greater than ourselves could restore us to sanity."[4] Ortberg summarizes this as confessing in our lives, "I can't" fix myself, but "He [God] can."[5]

NO FEAR NOW

In both the Gal 4 and the Rom 8 passages Paul emphasizes that one of the benefits of our adoption is that we need no longer be slaves of fear (Rom 8:15). "So why do we still fear?" we might ask ourselves, not imagining that the prodigal son in the story should fear his father after the very warm welcome home he received. Did that not solve their relationship hiccup? Or is fear always part of relating to an esteemed elder, in our case, to the high, holy

3. Ortberg, *Steps*, 9.
4. Ortberg, *Steps*, 33.
5. Ortberg, *Steps*, 280.

God? Even so, how could fear remain when the judge of all the earth has pardoned us and we have the privilege of praying to *Abba, Father*?

For Jewish readers learning from Paul of their adopted sonship status, their fear may have come from their cultural and religious background. They were steeped in the Old Testament Hebrew Scriptures and thought God so holy and his name so sacred that to write or even utter it was not practiced. Moreover, many of the covenantal rituals given to the Hebrews demanded separation from this holy God. Even faithful leaders like Moses, when given glimpses of God's glory, were warned not to presume on his majesty.

The Pharisees of New Testament days saw themselves as the religious gatekeepers of this divine holiness and insisted on extra rules and regulations, rules that people could not possibly keep in everyday life. In fact, the Pharisees themselves often did not keep them, but the rules only served to heighten their fear of a holy God. Jesus' fraught interactions with this religious group were often caused by his challenging their use of fear to maintain power over ordinary people. That was why Jesus countered their fear narrative by telling stories such as this one about the father with two sons. He was introducing them to God as a forgiving Father who makes a way for people to come home to love and acceptance without fear.

However, fear of intimacy with a holy God for the rest of us may be more like that of Paul's gentile hearers—internal fear—coming from an attitude to our own *self*, afraid of not being worthy of the astonishing blessings the Good Father offers. For example, the prodigal's guilt at squandering the family wealth on wild living may have been cleared by his father's welcome when he chose to come home, but does he forgive himself? Every time he looks at his father does he remember how much he hurt and disappointed him?

Unfortunately, most of us have lingering sadness and regret about our past, even though we have responded to the Father's call to turn and come home. We are assured, however, that our sonship is secure. The promise of inclusion in the family of God should be enough to set us free from this fear because "there is now no condemnation for those who are in Christ Jesus" (Rom 8:1). We will not be found unworthy or abandoned for we are God's forgiven sons and daughters.

FEAR FROM SHAME AS WELL AS GUILT

Fear is often associated with shame as well as guilt, however. Feelings of shame are a lead weight on so many of us, even though we know we are loved and accepted. I gave a whole chapter to describing the cause and effects of shame in my previous book.[6] At that time I was primarily referring to social shame, the kind that generates a false sense of self because of how we have been treated. Or shame that can arise from our despised status in society or in our family. I illustrated such social shame from my experience as a woman, but there are many ways people treat each other that give rise to shame—the "shame we don't deserve," Smedes calls it[7]—and we observe its consequences lingering long after a person enters a new standing with God as a son or daughter. These effects should not be dismissed but taken seriously and, if necessary, treated professionally. It may take time to heal, even with the ministry of the Holy Spirit and the support of compassionate and praying friends.

This was the shame we were addressing through the African program, Healing the Wounds of Trauma, described in chapter 3. The shame most of these women knew had its origins in how they had been treated, even abused, going back many years in some cases. Or through their circumstance as a widow or second wife, for example. But even though it was shame they did not deserve, many found relief in bringing their shame to Jesus' cross. They knew he had accepted their shame laid upon him and understood their condition. Their healing was furthered by sharing the experience with others around them and in the prayer partnering with another speaking their mother tongue that continued long after the conference.

THE PRODIGAL'S SHAME

There is, however, a shame we *do* deserve: the prodigal's shame. In an honor-shame society where relationships are so central, the young man in the story was clearly wrong to take his father and family for granted and spend his share of the estate in the way he did. Yet the shame of eating food with the pigs was finally a shame that drove him home—we might even call that a good shame! When we violate God's boundaries and rules for right living, we, too, should feel shame. But it does not need to linger or distort

6. Turner, *Finding Your Voice*, ch. 8 ("Beyond Shame").

7. Smedes, *Shame and Grace*.

our life for years to come. Finding we are freely and purposely adopted by God the Father offers us forgiveness and freedom from this kind of shame and relieves the fear caused by it.

If we can hardly believe it or are prone to forgetting our status as sons and daughters of the Good Father, we are invited to open our hearts to the Holy Spirit because "the Spirit himself testifies with our spirit that we are God's children" (Rom 8:16). In prayer and with support, we can consider our shame laid on Jesus, the Son who is publicly disgraced and hanging on the cross in our place. We might even be able to imagine the arms of the Son of God wide open, nailed to the cross, like the father's welcoming arms greeting the prodigal son as he neared home.

THE SPIRIT REMOVES FEAR

Feeling secure, unafraid, is a benefit of the Spirit's transformation our hearts need after we come home. It is a sign of our continuing spiritual growth that the Spirit of God takes away fear and reassures us that we are God's adopted and forgiven children. Entering this inheritance has many rich promises for sons and daughters, promises very familiar and precious to us from Rom 8: "The Spirit helps us in our weakness. . . . We know that in all things God works for the good of those who love him, who have been called according to his purpose. . . . We are more than conquerors through him who loved us. . . . Neither death nor life, neither angels nor demons, neither the present nor the future, nor any powers, neither height nor depth, nor anything else in all creation, will be able to separate us from the love of God that is in Christ Jesus our Lord." (Rom 8:26, 28, 37–39).

In the opening to the letter to the Ephesians there is another reference to adoption. Paul praises God for the spiritual blessings that we receive when we are in Christ (Eph 1:3–10). *In Christ* is a wonderful expression, summing up all that is now ours as the Father's children and coheirs with the Son—chosen, adopted, and loved.

Some years ago, I was commissioned by a publisher to write a resource for small groups based on the book of Colossians. Despite loving this Pauline letter, rich with imagery and insight into Jesus Christ, I never found a satisfactory expression in English to encompass the whole meaning of its key word: the *fullness* of God found in Jesus Christ. This fullness includes the power to fashion and sustain the universe, and so finally I thought *cosmic* would be a fitting epithet for Christ as Creator and Sustainer of everything and called the study The Cosmic Adequacy of Christ.

The wonder is that in Jesus Christ the *fullness* of God is not only cosmic but very down-to-earth. The Son from eternity took on human form to identify with us, rising from death in resurrection with power and pointing to our future resurrection. Because Jesus shares his humanity with us, his coheirs, we get a glimpse of the full potential of being human as was intended at creation. In our new status as sons and daughters, we know we are wanted and forgiven and so do not need to hide away in shame—we have the run of our inherited home, with Jesus the example of how to live as children of the Good Father. The perfect Son of God is our model of intimacy, obedience, and birthright.

Unfortunately, many of God's children consider it enough to just be home safely with the Good Father. They do not realize how great is their inheritance and so miss out on many of the benefits offered. We will explore some of these in the next chapter because in pondering the enormity of being the Good Father's children and coheirs with Jesus the Son, our expectation of what God through the Holy Spirit wants to do in our lives may be too low. But Paul reminds us, "Therefore, if anyone is in Christ, the new creation has come: The old has gone, the new is here!" (2 Cor 5:17). Home with the Good Father, growing more like Jesus, sharing with brothers and sisters also undergoing regeneration, we are a new family. There is so much more to understand, more to experience, more to appreciate of God in Christ and Christ in us. What does that look like? What is the family likeness we share? We need to uncover it.

RESPONDING

- If you can imagine Jesus looking at you, what emotion to do you see on his face? Disapproval? Disappointment? What does that tell you about how you think of yourself? Jesus' disciple Simon Peter knew the bitterness of disappointing his Master, denying he knew him in the courtyard after his arrest. Read John 21:15–19 and see how Jesus forgives and restores Peter.
- What qualities do you long for in your life now you are *in Christ*? Have you considered that these desires may be God-given, spurring you to

invite the Holy Spirit to renovate your heart to make you more like the Son of God?

- Is loving God and loving others a big challenge for you at the moment? What step of obedience is being asked of you to fulfill this dual command?

10

The Family Likeness: Becoming like Jesus

A disciple once asked his mentor if there was anything he could do to make himself grow spiritually. "As little as you can do to make the sun rise in the morning," he replied. When the disciple then wondered aloud what the value was of the spiritual exercises he was learning, the mentor answered: "To make sure you are not asleep when the sun begins to rise."

—Recounted by Leighton Ford, in Ruth Haley Barton, *Strengthening the Soul of Your Leadership*

Not long before his death in 2013, I was invited along with other former students and associates to a final conference with Dallas Willard in Santa Barbara, California. In one session, Willard was speaking about the possibility of daily growing more like Jesus. He asked those who desired this "renovation of the heart" to stand. All four hundred present stood, hungry to become more Christlike in character and to experience a deeper intimacy with God. For me, this welcome prospect came at a crucial time. I had just retired from an active working life and was finding that at retirement age, many of the things I enjoyed being and doing were dropping away. However, here I was discovering there was one thing that need not diminish or disappear as I got older. To the end of my earthly life, I could look forward to, indeed hunger for, a deepening relationship with God, becoming day by day more like Jesus in my attitudes and behavior. Moreover, at the end of the journey, an even more perfect union with God beckoned! Indeed, I was coming to see that my very hunger to grow more like Jesus was God-given.

When I think of Jesus' life as an example and impetus for mine, I long for his stability, his resilience, his love for others, his compassion, his self-sacrifice, his unquestioning obedience. So many practical things too: his ability to sleep (even in a storm); perspective on what was important and what could be let go; where to set boundaries; and how to build a sense of resting in the Father into a demanding life. I want to embrace who God has designed me to be, not experiencing shame nor being overly passive, and discover how to consistently put aside my own needs for the sake of others. Clearly, to be like Jesus will need ongoing work in my heart through the Holy Spirit all my earthly days, and I welcome that.

THE FAMILY LIKENESS

In the home of the Good Father, Jesus models for us the family likeness. His qualities of love, joy, peace, forbearance, kindness, goodness, and faithfulness are examples of the qualities of character the Holy Spirit wants to grow in us too. So how do we take on these characteristics? That is the question the disciple in the story at the beginning of this chapter asked his mentor, expecting to be given a list of activities or disciplines he could practice to achieve spiritual maturity. His mentor's response was a surprise, "Nothing!" Just as we cannot make the sun rise, we cannot manufacture spiritual depth. It is God's work in us. But we must be in the place to receive it.

Children learn from a parent by unconscious assimilation, and an apprentice develops skills by spending time with their Master; so we, too, can come to be like our model, Jesus, by spending time with him. We also grow like him by deliberately choosing to follow his way of life. In Jesus' earthly years, we see this centered around regular communion with the Father through solitude and prayer.

There are many ways to describe this process of becoming like Jesus and maturing into the family likeness, but the one I like best is *regeneration*. It includes healing as well as producing new growth from an inner reserve. Australians and others who live in Mediterranean-type vegetation understand this. We see how quickly our burned or drought-stricken trees recover and sprout new growth, *regenerating* after a wildfire or severe dry spell. The healing of our hurts and scars when we come home to the Good Father, which we discussed in chapter 3, can be the start of this regeneration. Another concept, *renovation*—used by Dallas Willard—we understand from multiple house improvement shows! We can apply it to Spirit-given change to our malformed and sin-shabby hearts.

In his letters to first-century churches the apostle Paul calls the gradual process of becoming like Jesus *formation*, or sometimes *transformation*, using the word for metamorphosis of a caterpillar into a beautiful butterfly. This is a useful concept because in life we do not stand still in the character-forming process. We are being transformed every day, one way or another, and not always in a godly direction. By our experiences, choices, thinking, influences (and influence-ers), we are being changed for good or ill. If we prefer to be a butterfly rather than a caterpillar, we must make metamorphosis a priority by letting the Holy Spirit form us into Jesus' likeness. This spiritual formation is what both the prodigal and the older son would have needed when or if they came home.

WE ARE BODY PEOPLE

The problem is that attaching "spiritual" to a change process, like spiritual regeneration or spiritual formation, can give the impression that becoming like Jesus makes us more ethereal beings and less bodily ones. But though he was God, Jesus was also a human being with a body. In fact, most of the things we celebrate about him involve his human body—his birth, his baptism, his death, his resurrection, his ascension. The way he touched people in healing them, or let people touch him, was through his "flesh and blood" body. He wept and ate and slept. He was like us in so many dimensions. Even after his resurrection and with a changed body, he had a physical presence with his disciples—in a house (John 20:26) or around a fire on the shores of Lake Galilee (John 21). As Willard says,

> The human body *is* the focal point of human existence. Jesus had one. We have one. Without the body in its proper place, the pieces of the puzzle of new life in Christ do not realistically fit together, and the idea of *really* following him and becoming like him remains a practical impossibility.[1]

1. Willard, *Spirit of the Disciplines*, 29–30.

Becoming like Jesus involves living as he did, in a human body. We are not purely ethereal spirits floating around. We need the facility of a body for life and interactions with people. Trying to shake off the body denies who Jesus was in his identification with us and in our modeling ourselves on him. "The body is the place of our direct power. It is our little 'power pack' that God has assigned to us as the field of our freedom and development,"[2] Willard explains, giving us the useful concept of the body as the *power pack* for the spirit. In our next chapter where we consider the significance of the promised resurrection of our bodies in the life after this life, we will see this distinctive Christian belief gives value to our bodies here as well as then.

Throughout the history of Christendom, there has been a stream of asceticism advocating separation from the real world and seeking mastery over the human body to earn God's favor. Taken to an extreme, that is a rejection of Jesus' message of *grace* which he wanted the Pharisees to hear as they watched and listened to his story of the father with two sons, the story of the prodigal coming home to God's love. Jesus' message to the Pharisees was that their pious and demanding way of life was not the way to God's approval. Rather, they needed to receive grace just like the tax collectors and "sinners" they despised who were also listening to Jesus that day.

We know that mastery in human life calls for discipline, the discipline of training, of building good habits and replacing destructive ones. Discipline is called for but not harsh asceticism. Rightly thought of, Christian disciplines are human body affirming, not body denying, because choosing some behaviors and not others distinguishes us from animals and robots and machines, especially ones controlled by AI! Above all, to be human includes having agency and making choices—that is, using the free will our Creator intended for us. But within that freedom, we must be willing to be called out by the Spirit whenever we try to live without reference to God, our Creator and Father.

LETTING THE HOLY SPIRIT CHANGE US

So if we cannot make ourselves more like Jesus, what is our role in this regeneration we need? It is to put ourselves in the place to receive God's transforming work, to rest in his grace. Paul describes the path, "We all, who with unveiled faces contemplate the Lord's glory, are being transformed

2. Willard, *Great Omission*, 89.

into his image with ever-increasing glory, which comes from the Lord, who is the Spirit" (2 Cor 3:18).

Because we are relational beings, any growth in personal qualities, including the so-called spiritual ones, will develop through interactions—primarily with God but with other people too. Relationships are central. As we have seen, Scripture reveals God—Father, Son, and Holy Spirit—to be like a circle dance, giving and receiving in mutual love and shared purpose, in unison. We are invited into the center of that. Our most fundamental relationship, this most incredible gift we have been given, is the invitation to relate to God in Jesus, becoming in the process more and more like Jesus. And whether we have been prodigal or coldly dutiful, responding to the Father's life-affirming "Welcome home!" begins the progression of change. And once we have begun to truly experience being loved and accepted and more like the first Son in the family, a hunger to keep on being changed into the likeness of Jesus will develop in us through the Holy Spirit (Eph 5:1–2).

The second picture we have of relating to the Good Father, our adoption as sons and daughters, has the same impetus for growing us in Godlikeness, for taking on the family likeness, and also starts from our relationship with the Father. We are not just guests in the family home, but by grace, we are his children now, with the right to be there. Through adoption, we receive security and safety enough to rest in the Father's love and make it our priority to seek the truly life-giving characteristics of Jesus, the first Son. The past is forgiven and we are being made whole; the healing of our hurts and scars has begun. We can even learn to trust enough to accept without complaint and with open hands the character changes he wants to bring. We can relish being no longer victims of past addictions and destructive habits; we can recover from what has been done to us. The renovation timetable may seem slow, but the Spirit often deals with issues one at a time, even though we would like him to just wave a magic wand and get it all done instantly!

Paul, writing to the Christians in the Roman city of Colossae about living as God's heirs and growing into the family likeness, describes this process of becoming like Jesus. We can think of this having three components—three angles of a triangle with the Holy Spirit the active agent at the center.

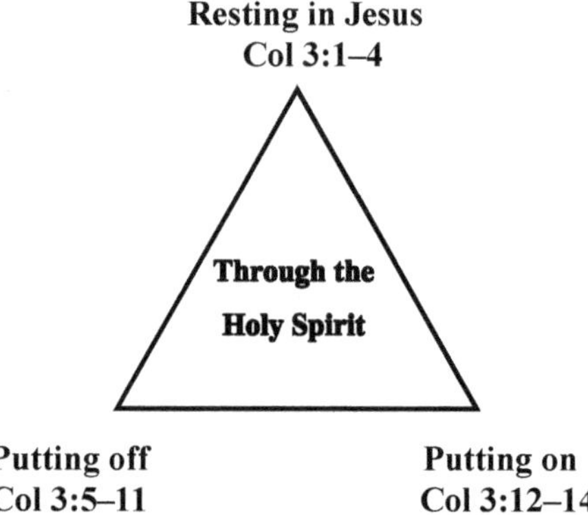

We start, Paul says in Col 3 (echoing 2 Cor 3:18), by cooperating with the Spirit and focusing on Jesus Christ, now seated in the place of authority with all resurrection power available to him. In acknowledging him, we gain perspective on what is happening in our world. We need have no fear because we are safeguarded (hidden) in Christ.[3]

> So if you're serious about living this new resurrection life with Christ, *act* like it. Pursue the things over which Christ presides. Don't shuffle along, eyes to the ground, absorbed with the things right in front of you. Look up, and be alert to what is going on around Christ—that's where the action is. See things from *his* perspective. (Col 3:1–2 MSG)

RESTING IN JESUS

The first angle—resting our hearts and minds in Jesus (Col 3:1–4)—means living in our new reality, what we are becoming. We are people being remade by the Holy Spirit's power. Though Paul gives this resting a future resurrection perspective, he is not advocating escape from the present physical world. Practical actions are very much in view because we live here and now, in human bodies, even though one day these bodies will be changed. A resurrection perspective gives us hope for the future without denying the reality of the present. As the way we are alive in this physical world, our bodies assist, or interfere with, the process of resting our hearts

3. In Colossians, a letter emphasizing Jesus' post-resurrection power and glory, Paul primarily uses Jesus' title *the Christ*.

and minds in Jesus and on our growth towards wholeness. The family likeness grows when we, with our physical bodies, deliberately establish patterns and rhythms that help us focus on Jesus and emulate him.

This is much more than holiness exercises requiring us to simply deny ourselves. That is just putting bars around the tigers. Unwanted desires and habits of living will still be tigers if they get out because rules and prohibitions are ineffective in dealing with the things that pull us down. Rather, learning "the unforced rhythms of grace" (Matt 11:29 MSG) causes us to look outside ourselves. Freed from excessive self-focus and instead following Jesus, we have the great privilege of enjoying a relationship with Father, Son, and Spirit forever.

Having taught about spiritual formation for many years in different cultures, I have found many Christians, discovering God's wonderful grace of acceptance and love, too quickly want to know what they can *do* to grow spiritually. That can easily cause them to try again to make themselves acceptable to the Father and earn his blessing by following a program. Rather, we must start from a *resting* position—*resting* in the Good Father's *grace* and letting the Spirit change us by responding to his corrections, promptings, and faith challenges as we gaze on Jesus Christ. There are many corners of our lives where we need to *rest* in Jesus, so we must come at this first angle from each of these.

The Rest of Home

"Repeating the atonement, not accepting it," someone has called the renewed striving to be acceptable. Life-changing *rest* in Jesus starts and continues when we no longer strive for our own salvation. Trying to earn acceptance with God was the Pharisaic disease which Jesus wanted to counter. In his story, the father waits patiently for the prodigal to come to the end of himself and turn for home; then his open arms speak of a grace-filled welcome. For the hardworking older son, the father offers this *rest* too. But the son must let go of his compulsive activity trying to prove his worth or earn his father's approval. Coming home would show his father loved him just as much as he loved his younger brother.

Whether we come as prodigals or older sons or daughters, it is the same for us. Now we are home, *rest* is luxuriating in the Father's grace. Because of Jesus' sacrifice, we can simply accept what God has done and say thank you. Coming home (or in) to the Good Father is *rest*, not because of anything we have achieved but solely because of the Father's mercy. Continuing to live in the Father's house and growing into the family likeness must be received as *rest* too because it depends just as surely on the Father's mercy. We can approach the demands of everyday life and responsibilities knowing we are not alone or on trial. "Come to me, all you who are weary and burdened," Jesus tells his followers, "and I will give you *rest*" (Matt 11:28; emphasis added).

The Rest of Confession and Forgiveness

One Saturday night some years ago we were having dinner at a neighbor's house and discussing over the meal the pressures of work. Two of the guests who had been raised as Catholics started to talk about the rest that comes from confession. A clean slate, a new start to the week, they called it. Another, a psychiatrist, admitted almost wistfully that he could not give that kind of relief to his patients. That *rest* is what we receive when we come home to the Good Father—the relief of being forgiven and a fresh start.[4]

The Rest of Not Hiding

There is wonderful *rest* in not having to hide who we really are. Keeping up a pretense is wearing and saps our vigor. In fact, in the presence of the Good Father it is a waste of energy because God's Spirit can penetrate any defense we put up to maintain a fiction about our own godliness. In the family with Jesus, we can relax and *rest*, not because we are perfect but because, as we have seen, Jesus has experienced shame and offers both an answer to our shame and a remedy for our sin.

We all know people who never relax when a visitor comes into their house. They are all too conscious of what is not clean or tidy, including what they intended to put right before it was seen. Their discomfort gets in the way of a relaxed conversation and sharing heart-to-heart. It need not be that way at home with Jesus, though the Spirit may have to do some repair work so that we abandon the habit of hiding.

4. Some material in this chapter first appeared in Turner, "He Gives His People Rest."

The Rest of Belonging

Now we have joined God's household, we have a new set of relationships among our brothers and sisters and with Jesus, the chief Son. In a society where loneliness is epidemic, the church community has many possibilities to provide acceptance and friendship to all comers. We dare not ignore these opportunities and turn away. We are called to belong to each other, to live in love, honoring one another and joining together in significant endeavors. If some past experience of hurt within a church has left its mark, surely the *rest* that comes from God's grace is wide enough to make belonging possible for us now.

The Rest of Enough

In industrial societies, rest is legislated with rules and boundaries, as it was for the Hebrews, to prevent exploitation of workers. When we lived in Manila, we discovered that laws for the protection of household servants were honored more in the breach than in the observance, and as I recounted previously, we had great difficulty convincing our maid we really wanted her to have her Sunday off to rest.

But the *rest* of enough is not so much a question of imposed economic exploitation for us in Western society today. We have, or could have if we shared it around, more than enough material things. It is no longer a question of Sunday prohibitions either, though for some self-employed businesspeople, Sunday trading hours are a matter of concern. But I have been startled to discover how often Old Testament prophets pointed to the abuse of the Sabbath rest as an indication that the people had forgotten their proper dependence on God. It always led to exploiting the land and abusing people. When their lives were in their own hands, getting at any price was the agenda for the Hebrews, and can be for us too.

Today the area where we probably most need the *rest* of enough is in the face of insistent calls for more and more activity: enough is enough! At least with regard to time, there are only twenty-four hours a day, so we must call a halt and make choices when we cannot fit any more activity in. Or forego the essential sleep our Creator has designed for our well-being. The problem is we feel either cheated or guilty about the choices we have to make.

When our sons were young, we told them they could not play a second sport each week. It would make our family too busy. They thought that most unfair because their friends played sports all weekend. Or more generally, when parents face a choice between vigorously pursuing a career or combining it with looking after children, they may feel cheated. Today we have an expression that sums up this aching for more: FOMO. Fear Of Missing Out. Why cannot we have it all? Peterson's paraphrase of Jesus' Sermon on the Mount applies to time as well as to other demands: "Steep your life in God-reality, God-initiative, God-provisions. Don't worry about missing out. You'll find all your everyday human concerns will be met" (Matt 6:33 MSG).

It is not a new challenge. Ernst Lange in 1970, reimagining in contemporary terms the fourth commandment to observe the Sabbath day, expressed it well:

> You don't need to run yourself to death!
> neither by uninterrupted work
> nor by an uninterrupted pursuit of pleasure
> neither by the worries you make for yourself—
> nor by the fear you may miss something
> All that makes you hopelessly cramped
> and takes away all joy in life.
> I, the almighty God want to be your master.
> Hold onto me, and your life will find fulfillment.[5]

If we are burned out or consumed with resentment about what is expected of us or what we cannot fit into our lives, we are not experiencing the *rest* of enough. It is time to stop and enjoy what God has given us, acknowledge our dependence on him, and start again in an incredible intimacy with the one who makes all things new.

Rest in the Easy Yoke

Jesus invited his disciples to come to him to rest with the words, "Take my yoke upon you and learn from me. . . . For my yoke is easy and my burden is light" (Matt 11:29–30). He was probably referencing the Palestinian tradition of plowing, which linked a younger animal to a more experienced one. Jesus reminds his followers, then and now, that when they are yoked with him, he takes the lead, shares the load, and demonstrates how to do it. The

5. Lange, *Ten Great Freedoms*.

pressures of family or work, health, or financial burden may not disappear, but they are shared with the Master.

In his book about eliminating hurry from our stressed lives, author and pastor John Mark Comer notes that in Jesus' day, *yoke* was the word used for a rabbi's unique teaching. It described the key to life that a rabbi taught his disciples. Jesus' special emphasis is that the yoke he shares with us is *easy*. In farming terms, a yoke is easy when it is well-fitting, made to exact specifications for comfortable use by the animal. Those who are yoked in teamwork to Jesus can expect an *easy* yoke because he knows us and what we need in the moment. He shares the load and teaches us how to live and serve with him. That truly is *rest*.

Dallas Willard once wrote on one of my books, "All joy and strength in the easy yoke." Perhaps he had sensed I was one of those older daughters still tending to work hard trying to earn God's approval. As Willard explains,

> The secret of the easy yoke is simple, actually. It is the intelligent, informed, unyielding resolve to live as Jesus lived in all aspects of his life, not just in the moment of specific choice or action.[6]

Choosing to live in the easy yoke with Jesus is not something we can just evoke in a crisis. It needs to be a settled way of living, *resting* in our relationship with him because we are building rhythms of prayer and contemplation in daily relationship with him.

The Rest of Completion

Biblical *rest* is about how we live, not by controlling or competing but with a sense of enjoyment and thankfulness for the life the Good Father has given us. God created for six days; on the seventh day he rested and enjoyed the fruit of his labor. The creation was good, it was finished, it was to be savored. That is the *rest* of completion.

Later, for the desert-wandering Hebrews, *rest* meant finally arriving at the land of promise and relaxing in safety under their own grapevine and fig tree (1 Kgs 4:25). Their objective attained, they could settle and enjoy it and give thanks. Grapevines and fig trees may be far from our contemporary day-to-day experience as places of *rest*, but there is a rural retreat center I visit which has both these symbols of agrarian satisfaction. There, the

6. Willard, *Spirit of the Disciplines*, 10.

grapevines and the fig tree remind me to *rest* in the Father and not spend the retreat time worrying about the demands on me that day or preparing for the next project.

Rest, even in the hard tasks God calls us to, is heard in God's promise to Moses commissioning him to once again pick up the heavy responsibility of leading a rebellious people: "My presence will go with you, and I will give you rest" (Exod 33:14). Clearly, *rest* for Moses (or us) is not idleness or avoiding challenge but a way of responding to everyday life demands.

PUTTING OFF OLD ATTITUDES AND HABITS

The second angle of the Holy Spirit's work in growing us into the family likeness calls us to deliberately *put to death* old attitudes and habits (Col 3:5–11). This "putting off" is to be a conscious action that we commit to, but it is second for a reason. It must grow out of *resting* in Jesus. Otherwise, it can turn into trying again to earn God's approval by making ourselves outwardly acceptable.

We have a picture of this from the history of the nation of Israel. Entering the promised land gave the Hebrews the satisfaction of having safely arrived, but it was not the end of their obligation to honor and obey their God. The writer to the Hebrews uses the idea of *rest* in the promised land to illustrate our position in Jesus and the obligation it brings: "Therefore, since the promise of entering his rest still stands, let us be careful that none of you fall short of it" (Heb 4:1). In the prodigal story scenario, God's promised *rest* requires us first to turn and come home. But living in the Father's house makes certain demands on our behavior, not to earn our right to be there—that comes from the Father's generosity and grace—but to honor the Father and accept responsibility towards those we share the home with. In other words, there are certain things we must not do, or get rid of, put off, now we are home.

Paul's first "put off" list specifies five kinds of sins which dishonor the Father. He starts with sexual ones but keeps his strongest condemnation for covetousness. Wanting something so badly that we will do anything to get it is worshiping the thing more than worshiping God and a direct affront to the Father who should have our first allegiance.

Then, using the mental image of getting rid of dirty old clothes, Paul turns to the question of how we use words and instructs us to "put off" using them hurtfully—whether in anger, irritability, envy, or with profanity.

Words may seem inconsequential compared to the other sins first mentioned, but they are like wild seeds blowing in the wind, sowing more pain, including for our brothers and sisters who are home with us.

Getting rid of the bad is more than self-control or New Year's resolutions, however. We must go to the root of the behavior in God's strength and recreative power. Recognizing evil—in the world, in the processes of human activity, and in ourselves—is the first step to freedom through Jesus. This "taking off dirty clothes" is a deep work we must let God prompt and enable in us.

Then, combined with the grace of self-control, we can live openly with one another. "Since you have taken off your old self with its practices" (Col 3:9) may be alluding to a custom of discarding their old clothes before being immersed in water through the ritual of baptism. It does not imply loss of personhood but rather leaving behind the former orientation which followed in the line of fallen humanity in order to put on a new orientation to the Creator. This process begins here and now as we are being restored to all God intended for us.

PUTTING ON THE GOOD QUALITIES

Thirdly, for the final angle of becoming like Jesus Christ, Paul again uses the baptism picture and urges followers to *clothe* themselves through the Spirit with compassion, kindness, humility, gentleness, and patience, replacing the old clothes they have put off with these clean ones (Col 3:12–14). It is essential when old ways and attitudes and habits are removed that they are changed for new ones. We know from experience that simply stopping something when it is harmful is not usually successful, unless the action or time slot or habit is replaced by another, more godly, one. This is probably what Jesus was warning about in a deeper sense when he said that by sweeping a room clean and leaving it empty, the vacuum would be filled by something worse (Matt 12:43–45).

Most gurus promoting a good life nominate one virtue they say binds everything together. For Jesus, that binding virtue is *love*. But love is the most self-giving, the most relational, the most demanding of all "new clothes," yet central because it is connected to everything! It is important to notice that the clean baptismal garments in Paul's illustration are ways of living and loving in Christian community, not just individual graces. God is re-Creator not only of the individual prodigal or older son but of the new family, the renewed sisters and brothers, adopted daughters and sons gradually taking on the family likeness. In pursuing personal wholeness, we dare not neglect working towards godly relationships. Growth for the individual often comes *through* rubbing shoulders in a caring community while it contributes *to* that community.

PREPARATION AND PRAYER

Paul's three angles on growing towards wholeness in Jesus rely on the work in us of the Holy Spirit but leave no room for personal complacency. The danger is that we will settle for too little. Spiritual growth and stability come from seeking it with all our heart and mind. Not only must our affections and wills be directed to Jesus but also our thinking transformed by Holy Spirit metamorphosis to take on God's alternative perspective.

There was an era when wearing a What Would Jesus Do (WWJD) wristband was popular. It was a useful reminder in decision-making that we have Jesus as our model and teacher. But as a slogan, it implies that all the wisdom and direction that is needed can arrive instantaneously, without preparation or training. Of course, with the Holy Spirit as our guide within, it is possible to receive immediately the understanding and courage that we need in the moment. The Father, who always listens for the cry of his children, will hear our urgent *arrow* prayers and respond in an appropriate way. But we also need as a way of life to prepare by prayer and listening to God well beforehand.

In his earthly ministry we see Jesus both praying in the moment but also spending time with the Father before undertaking the big challenges—choosing his disciples, mourning his cousin's murder, or starting off a final time for Jerusalem and certain death. His wisdom and actions in the midst of life were not just sudden insights or directions sent down via an instant hotline because he was God as well as a man. His preparation began in his years of twelve to thirty, hidden away in Galilee till his public ministry began, then continued in the three years of traveling around Palestine with his disciples as he set aside deliberate retreat times for prayer and ongoing consultation with God his Father.

Working in our easy yoke with Jesus must include such preparation too. A world-class athlete or swimmer does not reach their peak performance in the Olympic moment but after years of practice, hours of devotion to training, and expert coaching. For us, listening and growing like Jesus is a process that must go on to the end of our life.

PROMPTS FOR GROWING INTO THE FAMILY LIKENESS

In describing how we take on the family likeness in this chapter, I have deliberately avoided using the term *spiritual disciplines* because Jesus' story of the father offering love and acceptance to his two sons is the very opposite of earning God's approval by doing or not doing certain things. I also have not wanted to lay out a program for becoming like Jesus that is prescriptive, as if we can follow it without the personal relationship with God we were created for and for which he seeks us out—that gift of incredible intimacy he offers us. What the Spirit does in our lives and where he leads us individually is tailored to us personally, and maybe not what we would choose if it was left to us. But when we turn for home and enter the house of the Good Father, we are coming under his wonderful care and must make sure we are open to receive the transformation that begins then and continues to the end of our earthly life.

Richard Foster, Dallas Willard, John Ortberg, Robert Mulholland, and Ruth Haley Barton have been my spiritual guides in seeking to grow more like Jesus, but there are many other resources available to guide this formation. What is important, however, whatever we pursue in life-changing practices, is to do it from a position of *rest*, firstly setting our hearts and minds through the Holy Spirit on Jesus because we are at home with the Good Father.

MODELING RELATIONAL INTIMACY TO OUR SOCIETY

There is another important aspect to this taking on the family likeness, one for others, not just for ourself. Today our fractured and lonely society also needs people who have experienced coming home to the Good Father to model healthy relationships, to deliberately make connections, and to share life in the wider community. We know that humans are created in the image of the relationship God—the three-in-one Father, Son, and Holy Spirit. We know we are more than animals, more than robots, more than machines.

We know we function best not by expressing our individualistic self but in relationship with others. We are made for relating, made for belonging. Isolation from other human beings in a fearful Christian "ghetto" is the opposite of the Creator's intention. All human beings are his creation, all on his heart, and all hungry for relationships. Coming home to the Good Father gives us the experience of connection and love, but it also calls us to show how it is transforming our lives and enabling us to serve others.

Of course, the biological family is the primary level of relating. In the origin statements of Gen 1 and 2 we read that of the first man God said, "It is not good for the man to be alone." He gave him a counterpart, a woman, to form the first family (Gen 2:18–25). Our connection is firstly to our Creator, then to our immediate family, then to those we share our church community with, but also to the people where we have been placed—neighborhood, work, sporting team, other associations. This is for their good as well as for our own. In whatever way we share with them the God who reveals himself in Jesus, we will want them to know the delight of being loved by their Creator who beckons them home.

BEING COUNTERCULTURAL

Historians have examined the first few centuries of the Christian era to find an explanation for the surprisingly rapid early growth of the Christian church. They credit it to the actions of the ordinary, mostly modest individuals and families who influenced a whole empire by their countercultural contribution to society, especially during times of plague. The Roman world was difficult for Christians. They were rejected and ridiculed, sometimes persecuted, and called all sorts of names. But as historian Rodney Stark observes, this "obscure, marginalized Jesus movement became the dominant religious force in the Western world in a few centuries."[7]

The widespread plagues in these centuries were a serious matter, especially in the late fourth century when up to 30 percent of Roman citizens died. But in these plagues the early believers witnessed and served by being countercultural. While anyone with any means within the empire "ran for the hills" out of fear of infection, the Christians stayed and cared for their neighbors, sometimes losing their lives in doing so. Similarly, when unwanted girls and disabled babies were exposed and left to die, Christians rescued them, adopting them into their families. And when Roman society

7. Stark, *Rise of Christianity.*

treated women as property to be used or abused, Christians were taught they were equal partners in marriage (1 Pet 3:7). Well-known Australian journalist Greg Sheridan draws attention to this valuing of marriage by early Christians, arguing it was good for the men as well as the women.[8]

Moreover, when the surrounding society considered them unworthy because it was their fault that they were needy, widows and other destitute people were supported through the church community. This led Christians in later centuries to be in the vanguard of establishing orphanages, hospitals, hospices, schools, and other social supports wherever they went. Clearly these persecuted Christians were heeding the apostle Peter's words: "Live such good lives among the pagans, that, though they accuse you of doing wrong, they may see your good deeds and glorify God on the day he visits us" (1 Pet 2:12).

The contemporary epidemic in Western society is not biological plague but loneliness. So how are we reaching out in friendship to the people around us? Offering hospitality and inclusion is both a personal challenge and one for our church communities.

COMMUNAL INTIMACY

When we earlier focused in chapter 2 on the incredible intimacy we are invited into by the Good Father, we thought of it as a personal experience, as is our usual Western habit. And in one sense our spiritual journey is always personal, and not just in individualistic societies such as ours. Even in honor-shame cultures where a man or woman's needs and desires are expected to be subjugated to the good of family and society, the decision to come home to God must be a personal one. In the society where Jesus told his two-sons story, family and societal obligations loomed much larger than in ours, but both sons in the narrative were free to choose their different paths, despite family obligations. Similarly, Jesus' call to the people he met, including the wealthy ruler (Luke 18) or the despised tax collector (Luke 19), was just like the invitation to his first twelve followers, a personal one.

Yet when we discover the love of *Abba*, our waiting *Father*, we discover that we are not a sole follower, but there are many others around us. We are God's daughters and sons in a big family. The apostle Paul goes so far as to say that by faith we are included in the children of Abraham (Gal 3:26–28). Being Christian is a higher identity than our ethnic, social, or

8. Sheridan, *How Christians Can Succeed*, 59.

gender differences, though these continue to be our human characteristics. He reiterates this same message to the church in Rome, a very diverse mix of people (Rom 8:16).

As a woman marginalized in church life in earlier years by my gender, these Galatian and Romans verses have been reassuring regarding my standing before the God who created, redeemed, and gifted me to serve, but they have much wider application in communal church practices, as well as in society generally. Martin Luther King Jr. called 11:00 a.m. Sundays the most segregated hour in American life. King was speaking about this in the 1960s, and church service times and modes now are more varied, but divides of age, generation, and ethnicity, as well as denominational emphases, still exist.

In the church I pastored up to my retirement, we had an influx of Christian South Sudanese refugees into our suburb. So we hosted a separate congregation where the older Dinka generation could sing and hear in their mother tongue while school-age children who were learning English were able to be included in the general congregation. We made some lasting friendships among the families before the majority moved for more permanent housing to outer suburbs and away from our location. As I ponder the importance of experiencing and demonstrating the oneness that is ours as heirs of the Good Father, I now think we should have worked and prayed harder to integrate our two congregations. We sisters and brothers in the family of God have a mandate to display our oneness in Christ and love for one another for all to see. Our loving is not self-generated but comes because we first have been loved by God. Surely his love to us can overflow to a society that drives division between people groups and generations.

Meanwhile, to use still another metaphor, the sons and daughters of the Good Father are together being made into Jesus' beautiful bride. What a prospect! That must be the theme of our next chapter.

RESPONDING

- There is a saying: "Sitting at a piano does not create a masterpiece, but you had better be sitting at one when the creative impetus arrives!" How does that illuminate the story at the head of this chapter? How does it fit with the description in Colossians 3 of how to grow spiritually?

- "Learn the unforced rhythms of grace," is Peterson's *The Message* paraphrase of Matt 11:28. Can you identify a grace rhythm you want to *put on* in place of a habit or attitude you know you should *put off*? Reading the Colossians 3 lists will provide some examples.
- Does *resting* in Jesus through the *easy yoke* speak to you where you are in your life? What will you do about it? And how will that be countercultural in your community?

11

Is Heaven Home?

We have multitudes of professing Christians who may well be ready to die but obviously are not ready to live, and can hardly get on with themselves, much less with others.

—Dallas Willard, *The Great Omission*

As dawn approached one Easter Sunday my husband and I were traveling across Perth in a taxi to the airport, on our way overseas yet again. The sun was just starting to lighten the sky as we drove towards it—a giant ball of fire in the east. I thought of those women walking to the tomb in Jerusalem on that Easter Sunday long ago, using the first light of the day after the Sabbath to anoint the crucified body of their beloved Master. That morning in their grief, did they notice the little jump the rising sun makes as it comes above the horizon—the *day spring*? In Luke's birth narratives, Jesus is called "the dayspring from on high" (Luke 1:78 KJV). *Dayspring* is a word full of promise, of new beginnings, and Luke is using it to remind us of the future promise focused on Jesus the Christ who came to live among us.

To their great surprise those women found the tomb empty. They did not know it yet, but Jesus was alive. When I ponder why I am a follower of Jesus, it is his resurrection that both moves and convinces me. Many good people have been killed for a high cause. Martyrs, we call them. But it is not just his life or death that makes Jesus a hero and the focal point of history—it is his resurrection that affirms he has conquered evil. And surely death is the greatest challenge of all!

This was one martyr raised to life again—a sure sign that he is God with us today in a wonderfully accessible way. We may ponder *why* Jesus had to die on our behalf and harness many different metaphors to explain *how* his death and resurrection is the answer to our alienation from our Creator and from ourselves. But we do not need to know how it works, only trust the one who did it and orient our life to him to walk in the wonderful relationship he offers.

THE IN-BETWEEN SATURDAY

The Saturday before the resurrection Sunday must have been a terrible nightmare for Jesus' first followers. They believed so ardently in his mission yet saw him die before it could be realized. They did not know that the next dawn would bring back their Master, risen from the dead.

I have never been good at in-between times. If we plan something, I want to put it into action straightaway. If it is time to say goodbye after an enjoyable evening with friends, I want to do it simply and quickly, then go out the door. When my husband and I were contemplating the next stage of where to live beyond our working years, we decided it was best to downsize while we were still active and could manage the work involved in getting established in a new house. We would move to where we could live indefinitely, make new friends, adjust to a new pace of life, and later bring in some support services if we needed assistance.

So we made the decision, fixed up and sold the big house, and quickly moved into a smaller villa with no stairs and reduced maintenance, all in just a month or two. The speed of our downsizing surprised even our family! We just wanted to get on with it, not knowing when age decline would appear or how urgently frail-age support would be needed.

We were living within an *Easter Saturday*. Good Friday was saying goodbye to all the things my husband and I could do in our prime but no longer—climb mountains, travel the world, do cutting-edge science, lead a church, welcome new grandchildren and kick a ball with them as they got older. But what would come next? We knew the wonder of Jesus making sense of our reality to this point, and we had been granted a good life. But death was coming, and before resurrection to a fuller hereafter, what would the rest of our earthly life be. Dementia? Physical incapacity? We have seen what that means. Both our mothers were cared for by their husbands through infirmity for eight long years before their deaths. Would our final days be like that too? Or would it be the other way around—my caring for my husband who is several years older than me? In the uncertainty of these years before passage to the next life, we need *Easter Saturday* to speak to us of trusting God's loving hands without knowing how it will work out.

In fact, the *not yet* of an Easter Saturday can teach us many things—valuable because in the bigger picture, we are living in the *not yet* before Jesus returns to bring in the fullness of his rule. These years have worth in themselves because God is in all time and space. He created it! But compared to those first bereft disciples, we are in a much better place to seize the moment because we know that Easter Sunday with all its promise has already come. Jesus has been raised and that signifies our future too. Those who follow in the footsteps of their Resurrection Lord can rightly be called resurrection people, or Easter people, because the resurrection (Christ's and ours to come) influences all we are and do now, as well as in the future.

There is much we do not know about the next life, and the Scriptures give us little detail, but we do know that it centers around our relationship with God the Father through Jesus. We are assured that the relationship we have now at home with the Good Father will continue in the hereafter and be even more intimate and perfect. So while we savor his love now, we rightly long for an even more complete union, face-to-face with Jesus.

FARTHER UP AND FARTHER IN

In his Narnia stories, C. S. Lewis imaginatively illustrates this both now and future relationship with God. Throughout the seven books, the children (and animals) have met Aslan, the welcoming but majestic lion king. They have known his care and strength and self-sacrifice and can think of nothing better than being with him in Narnia. Yet it is not until they respond to the call to go "farther up and farther in" (in the last book of the series) that they understand how everything on their previous visits to Narnia was just a taste of the real, all-encompassing reality they are now experiencing, and this reality has no ending. In Lewis's words,

> It was the unicorn who summed up what everyone was feeling. He stamped his right fore-hoof on the ground and neighed, and then cried: "I have come home at last! This is real country! I belong

> here. This is the land I have been looking for all my life, though I never knew it till now. . . . Come farther up, come farther in![1]

We, too, are invited to come farther up and farther into communion with God. The relationship that we have already experienced stretches into a future of even greater delights. This is the biblical understanding of hope, anchored in Jesus' resurrection but consummated in the future return of Jesus, at his "second" coming.

What is important is that this promise of a future resurrected life does not deny or replace the wonderful intimacy of being at home with the Father possible here but rather is an intensification of what we have already tasted. Nor is it a rejection of this present God-created world. These are two issues of significance which we must address when we think about heaven. One is how we live in our human bodies now; the other is our concept of future bliss.

CARING FOR OUR BODIES

Being resurrection people means we can have a positive attitude to our own bodies here and now because the prospect of resurrection reassures us that they will not be eternally discarded but renewed in some wonderful way by their Creator. The apostle Paul illustrates this by pointing to the continuity between a wheat seed and the plant that springs from it. For human bodies, is this continuity of appearance? Personality? Relationships? In this not-yet time, that is not clear to us, but it certainly does not imply rejection. In fact, Paul uses this valuing of God-created human bodies to argue for care and integrity in the use of them now (1 Cor 6:12–15).

I remember standing with my father and brother by my mother's bed as she breathed her last. She had experienced many years of physically wasting away, and that night in her nursing home she was a shadow of her former self. Death, when it came, was a release. As we caught our breath in the corridor outside her room, we processed the "passing over" we had just witnessed and comforted each other with the words, "Next time we see her, she will again be in her prime."

What is the physical prime of life? Forty, fifty, or, as some early church fathers suggested, thirty, the age at which Jesus began his ministry? It does not matter when we have the promise that in union with Jesus we will

1. Lewis, *Last Battle*, 243.

somehow be fully restored in a resurrected body, all we were created to be. The older we get, as the aches and pains mount up, the more treasured is this expectation, but our attitude to our God-created personhood and physical appearance also needs to be appropriate to our age and where we are in the life cycle. It is not realistic to expect to look forty-five years old at seventy nor reasonable to go to extraordinary lengths to prolong life. Our future prospect of heaven helps us live with limitations now because, however much we have neglected our bodies or others have mistreated us, we are not outside of God's love and care in this not-yet time before resurrection.

Theologian Scot McKnight, in his book addressing the many questions people have about transition to the next life, suggests that when facing death, we should picture ourselves standing in Jesus' empty tomb.[2] The tomb is empty because Jesus has been raised from death, so it speaks wonderfully to us of our promised resurrected future, face-to-face with him, and reminds us that the power that raised him to life again can do that for us too (1 Cor 6:14, Eph 1:18–21).

FUTURE BLISS

When life is difficult it is tempting to think the only relief available is in the future, up there, away from earth, beyond death. This causes some Christians to want to get out, escape to a better place and not worry about this world, supposing it is going to be discarded. Such thinking leads to neglect of our planet and its people, to even choosing to contribute recklessly to the earth's pollution and degradation. Yet stewarding God's creation was a mandate given to those made in God's image at the beginning, and the mandate still applies. N. T. Wright emphasizes the connection between earth and heaven in his observation, "You only really know God and share his life when you understand that he is the creator and lover of earth just as much as of heaven."[3]

In other words, how we picture our ultimate destiny matters because it influences decisions and actions now. Utopias are important, not because they can be realized but for what they express of our highest aspirations. They affect how we live and what we work towards. Think of doctors facing a crowded waiting room day after day but dreaming of a paradise free of

2. McKnight, *Heaven Promise*, 16.

3. Wright, *Surprised by Hope*, loc. 4550.

needy people. It could make them unduly irritated with their patients. Or economists who envision a financial market uncomplicated by the behavior of consumers; or designers of computer systems who would rather not take into account the idiosyncrasies of the people who will use their programs; or teachers whose love of their subject makes them long for receptive blank slates instead of the complicated young people who fill their classroom. Imagining that life and work would be more straightforward if we could just jet out of here affects how we treat individuals, especially if our primary desire is to shake off these less-than-perfect people or our world.[4]

This is why our picture of heaven is important. If we long for heaven to be a place to get away to, one without humans except for our nearest and dearest, one just focused on a peaceful existence, then we can become impatient with people and our circumstances here. Moreover, if we focus solely on heaven as our future goal, we will miss much of what our Creator wants us to be doing here and now. After his essential teaching on resurrection and the future, the apostle Paul brings the focus back to the present and relates it to the Corinthians' current life in this world with the words, "Therefore, my dear brothers and sisters, stand firm. . . . Always give yourselves fully to the work of the Lord, because you know that your labor in the Lord is not in vain" (1 Cor 15:58). Today for us, too, our current living space is not an idle waiting room but an arena for actively following Jesus our Lord.

ESCAPE TO PARADISE?

"Going home" is one way people commonly describe passing into life-after-life for Christians, but that expression can mislead. The prodigal son hearing his father's "Welcome!" did not need to wait till death to be home. If we, too, have responded to the Father's invitation, God's love and acceptance are ours now. They do not wait for another world somewhere up there, in a paradise with clouds floating and harps sounding.

Paradise is a word often used by people to suggest what heaven is like. Sometimes, I ask people about their idea of it. A few do respond with those images of harps and clouds, but most dream of green fields, flowers, and peaceful woods, perhaps with birds singing or wind whistling gently through the trees. Those with ears attuned to nature may describe a gurgling stream or the crunch of dried leaves. In dry and arid Australia, one

4. Some material in this chapter first appeared in Turner, "Paradise a City?"

of our favorite sensations is the smell of new rain on dry dirt, so perhaps a sense of smell, said to be the most enduring of human senses, is involved in our idea of paradise! But few in any Western culture mention the presence of other people in paradise, except perhaps family members. No one has ever told me they picture a *crowd* of people in a *built* environment!

This is understandable. Though rarely used in Scripture, *paradise* is a Greek word of oriental origin meaning a pleasure park full of the beauties of nature. Many people associate it with the garden of Eden described in the first chapter of Genesis. So they imagine the paradise of heaven as a return to Eden—to peace, tranquility, and escape from the pressures and evils of human life as we know it. How wonderful that would be!

Many times, the Scriptures represent peace and satisfaction with physical imagery. We noted previously how rest in the Hebrews' promised land was pictured as relaxing under your own fig tree or grapevine. Earlier, God had given them, through Moses, festivals to celebrate the bringing in of the year's harvest. The beauty of trees and flowers and full ears of grain are a gift from the Creator who enjoys their beauty and fruitfulness too. A verdant tree of life thread can be traced through Scripture, beginning in the first garden, with many mentions along the way, before reappearing as a life-giving tree in the last book of the Bible. But if we imagine heaven as a return to a distant Eden to escape this marred world, we are not honoring the Creator and Redeemer of planet Earth. He has plans for Eden's restoration in a new picture.

In any case, the essence of Eden is not the setting, as beautiful as it must have been, but the relationship with its Creator. Before sin came, the garden was where God walked in fellowship with the first man and woman. It was where he invited them into stewardship of his wonderful world. And where then he made his promise of redemption for sinful people and for his creation.

A HEAVEN-ON-EARTH CITY

The biblical end-time version of ultimate joy and delight turns out to be a surprise, not a garden but a *city* teeming with people—new Jerusalem "coming down out of heaven" (Rev 21:2). It is a place of restored relationships, firstly with its Creator but also with his redeemed people "from every nation, tribe, people and language" (Rev 7:9) and with his world—a city beautiful, and holy, and populated!

The reason this heaven-picture is a surprise in many cultures, including ours, is that we equate cities with loss of morality, not with purity and completeness. I remember in a university seminar on rural depopulation discussing whether country people were more moral than their city cousins. Certainly, where cities are the result of recent internal migration, their residents do not have the safeguards of traditional and common mores or the daily scrutiny of behavior that settled, clan-based communities have. City dwellers are freer in their anonymity to act as they please and associate with whom they like. And they do.

As a former city planner, the word *city* has a particular resonance for me, particularly when in the 1960s we resided in an American city and were very involved in advocating through our church for the welfare of its neglected slum residents living around us in poverty. Our congregation would even defiantly sing a hymn that began, "God of concrete, God of steel." But despite our congregation's strong urban commitment, we still harbored a residual association of human society with evil when we looked at the nearby slums, and we still longed for a place of untouched nature as our image of heaven. Moreover, as a planner I knew that when it came to finding land for greatly needed new houses, or workplaces for underemployed urbanites, being *for* nature usually led my clients to be *against* people and their jobs coming into their suburbs.

In the United States, this anti-city bias goes back at least to Thomas Jefferson, who declared great cities "to be pestilential to the morals, the health and the liberties of man."[5] In Australia, we are more ambivalent. Looking at the proportion of the population who live in urban centers, we are one of the most urbanized nations in the world. Yet we still consciously identify with the *bush* and the supposed resilience, self-sufficiency, and improvising character it has produced in us. Few of us willingly call ourselves city lovers.

No wonder heaven is thought of as a paradise, as a garden to which to escape, and not a city.

SCRIPTURE'S CITY IS RESTORED

Distrust of what the *city* represents is not just a cultural preference but a wider biblical theme too, as Jacques Ellul explains.[6] Because a city is inherently the physical expression of complex human relationships when large

5. Jefferson to Benjamin Rush, Sept. 23, 1800.
6. Ellul, *Meaning of the City*.

numbers of people live side by side, it follows that when city dwellers and their relationships are corrupted by wrongdoing, the city itself takes on an aura of evil—more people means more possibility of evil. The symbolism in the Bible makes this is clear. Cain built the first city as a substitute for his loss of family relationships (Gen 4), for example, and the builders of Babel with its tower to the sky saw it as a sign of their independence from God (Gen 11).

So when the imagery of the book of Revelation depicts the renewed earth and heavens as a city, a new Jerusalem coming down to earth, it is of great significance. It tells us that the Creator has taken the very vehicle of human rebellion and remade it into a vision of hope. We can read it as more evidence that the Creator refuses to turn his back on us. He does not reject the city as we do because it represents, even breeds, alienation and distrust and despair. He does not say, "You people always make a mess of your relationships. Go on your way alone." Rather, as the Good Father, he continually offers to restore fellowship—with himself and with others and with the natural world. So his promised relationship has its ultimate expression in a beautiful city speaking of perfect communication and love for the whole world, nature included. That promise for the future is expressed in Revelation as no pain or tears, no loneliness, no misunderstanding, no fear, no competition, no distrust, no envy, no bitterness. Only renewal and reconciliation (Rev 21:1–4).

This new Jerusalem is the restoration of what was lost in the garden of Eden. At its center is Jesus, fulfilling God's promise of the life-renewing "seed" descended from the first erring humans (Gen 3:15 KJV). Furthermore, the heavenly city coming to earth is holy because its inhabitants are made holy by a holy God. It is built of and for people who through turning back are reconciled to God and to one another; they are the resurrected sons and daughters, brothers and sisters, in God's family. This *people* restoration is its focus, but as in the first Eden sinful actions had consequences for all of creation, so restoration through Jesus affects all. The new Jerusalem will incorporate a beautiful, renewed earth.

HEAVEN HAS ALREADY BEGUN

It is worth saying again. The danger in picturing heaven only as a home of escape in the future diminishes our expectation and enjoyment of a relationship with God here and now. Like *going home*, the words *finally at peace* are another expression often used in connection with a person's death. Of course, in face of death, and especially if the loved one's final days of earthly life have been a struggle, it is understandable that what we want for them (and for ourselves) is peace at that time. The problem is that desire implies that rest for them is possible only somewhere beyond current earthly experience.

That belief is also why bereaved people often take comfort in imagining their loved ones watching over them from above. I have heard this said by family members at funerals and is reflected in a practice of Australian cricketers. Recently, a promising young player was felled by a very fast cricket ball bowled at him. At significant milestones in the games that followed, his fellow players have lifted their bats to gesture to the heavens, acknowledging their mate looking down and cheering them on.

To overcome people's expectation that heaven is up there, outside this world, far beyond present reality and only in our future, my theologian father suggested not using the word *heaven* but adopting Paul's use of the adjective form of the word and talking about *the heavenlies*, meaning the spiritual sphere where God reigns (Eph 1:3, 20; 2:6; 3:10; 6:12). *Heavenlies* suggests not a place but a spiritual dimension which we can enter now in fellowship with the Father. In Wright's words, "Heaven, in the Bible, is not regularly a future destiny but the other, hidden dimension of our ordinary life—God's dimension."[7]

Similarly, John Stott in his commentary on Ephesians draws attention to Paul's use of the expression and describes it as "neither sky, nor grace, nor glory, nor any literal special abode, but rather the unseen world of spiritual reality."[8] That is the realm we are invited into *now* by our Good Father through prayer. Some reject such a relationship with God as not possible or real or wanted. But if it is not wanted now, it is reasonable to ask why they would desire or be comfortable with connection to God in a future life! There is continuity for created people with their Creator which cannot be escaped.

In other words, heaven—that is, *the heavenlies*—is already available in this not-yet time. Jesus' resurrection has inaugurated a new era, God's kingdom here on earth, which will be fully realized when Jesus returns physically. Whether we are prodigals or older sons, home is already ours when we turn back into the Father's waiting arms. Rest, too, is available now, not

7. Wright, *Surprised by Hope*, loc. 684.

8. Stott, *Ephesians*, 35.

only in the hereafter, because Jesus offers the *easy yoke* in the midst of a life lived in tandem with the Master. Moreover, we do not need to get out of here to be with sisters and brothers in our God-given family. We know it may not be perfect fellowship in the present because we are still being transformed into the family likeness of Jesus, still being healed of hurts and scars, and still learning to be reconciled with one another. But Christian community here in the church can be full of promise and encouragement and worth working towards, a taste of heaven.

McKnight in his book about heaven describes in some detail the death of Dietrich Bonhoeffer[9] to illustrate how being face-to-face with Jesus in the hereafter is a continuation beyond bodily resurrection of the relationship with God possible here and now. Of Dallas Willard's death in 2013, a friend remarked that such was the closeness of his ongoing walk with Jesus in this life that he might not have immediately noticed he had passed over into the next!

So we might summarize the biblical picture of God's realm, *the heavenlies*, as more *relationship* than *place*. We are invited into it here and now through the redeeming work of Jesus. We experience being seen, loved, and cared for now, even though the welcome will be even more wonderful one day, face-to-face. In Willard's words,

> We need not and must not wait until we die to live in the land of milk and honey; and if we will only move to that land now, the passage in physical death will be but one more day in the endless life we have long since begun. That is exactly what Jesus meant when he said, "If anyone keep my words he shall never see or taste death."[10]

The burden of Willard's lifelong teaching was that delaying till we die to know the rich relationship with God we were created for is a Great Omission and a great loss. It is an omission in the way we are being trained as apprentices of Jesus, and it distorts the way we obey the Great Commission in calling others to follow Jesus. The gospel tells us we can have that fellowship now. Why wait to urge people to "get over the line" of faith until just before they die when they could be living their remaining earthly days at home with the Good Father as well as transition into life with God in an even more wonderful way after death and their resurrection?

9. McKnight, *Heaven Promise*, 52–53.

10. Willard, *Renovation of the Heart*, loc. 515; his paraphrase of John 8:51.

TASTE HEAVEN NOW

When Jesus prayed for his disciples the night before his death, he longed that their relationship would continue. He gave no details of what their reunion would look like, only that their Father was preparing a place for them to be together again (John 17:24). He is assuring them that it is continuing connection that matters, not the location.

So if heaven is in essence our relationship with God (and the other sons and daughters) and can begin here and now, why wait? Why try to live without the incredible intimacy the Good Father offers, without the healing of hurts and scars, without access to prayer, without daily awe overcoming dangerous self-absorption? Why spurn the welcoming arms, the release from accusing perfectionism offered to older sons, and the opportunity to be daughters and sons together in God's family alongside the first Son? Why not become more like Jesus in an existence that will continue seamlessly after physical death? Why not let the hope of redeemed and resurrected bodies influence how we relate to this planet and its people? Why not choose life now in all its intended fullness? Taste heaven in this liminal moment!

RESPONDING

- What picture of heaven have you inherited from your culture and family history? How does it compare with the few glimpses of heaven the Scriptures give us? If it is only a future concept for you, how does it connect to your life here and now?
- Funeral services traditionally included reference to "a sure and certain hope of the resurrection to eternal life," but it is heard less frequently now. What value will it be for you when you are facing your own death to picture yourself, as suggested by Scot McKnight, standing in Jesus' empty tomb and knowing resurrection is for you too?
- Heaven is a continuation and enhancement of the incredible intimacy we can have now with the Good Father in *the heavenlies*. Are you experiencing that, and are you looking forward to an even greater personal and shared relationship in the future life-after-life?

12

This Liminal Moment

We must pay the most careful attention, therefore, to what we have heard, so that we do not drift away.

—Hebrews 2:1

There is a shipwreck just off the coast of our city easily accessible to snorkelers, even ones like us who do not venture far from the shore. We explored it one weekend. The largely submerged wreck, the iron ship *Omeo*, in 1905 was nearing the end of its cargo-carrying life and moored in the nearby port of Fremantle, but its anchor did not hold. It drifted till it stuck fast in the sand of a nearby beach. All weekend after we had surveyed its crusted hull and remaining iron mast, I had the old tune echo through my mind, "Will your anchor hold in the storms of life?" The snippets of the song make it sound as if it is up to us to ensure our anchor in life is a good one. And in one sense, that is our responsibility. We have a choice about what we depend on to give us meaning and stability over the years. But our steadiness, our ability to persevere, does not depend on our determination to last the distance but on the anchor we depend on for that journey. The *Omeo* was a strong ship, but its anchor failed, and so it drifted. The writer to the Hebrews reminds his readers (and us) that Jesus is our secure anchor, our source of hope (Heb 6:19). We need that anchor of hope so we do not drift.

THIS LIMINAL MOMENT

> Liminal: of, relating to, or being an intermediate state, phase, or condition.
> —*Merriam-Webster* Dictionary[1]

A liminal moment is not ambiguity but a divide between two states. It is like standing on the threshold of a new chapter of life—an uncertain chapter but one full of potential. It is not the beginning of the story nor the ending but the middle chapter. Something like the challenge of an Easter Saturday.

As we wait for the full realization of the wonderful future Easter Sunday which follows, we must recognize the liminal moment we are in. If we have come home to our Good Father, a fulfilling life in Jesus is already available to us through the Spirit, but we have a further choice. How will we live the rest of our life? How will we continue in this world which still awaits the complete restoration of all God has promised? All is not rosy yet.

SEIZE THE HOPE

Facing a health challenge a few years ago, I was confronted with the thought that maybe my life here was done. Was it time to be, in the apostle Paul's words, "with Christ"? Though in many ways that was a welcome prospect, I felt encouraged to hang on, not only to see my grandchildren grow up but also for the sake of those to whom I am mentor and teacher. And as companion to my husband.

But my death threat was nothing like that faced by many Christians in the first centuries after Jesus' earthly ministry, or today in Pakistan, Iraq, Egypt, or Niger, where fear of death is matched by fear of physical and mental torture. That degree of pressure to give up or hide one's faith is something we in Western countries can hardly imagine. The danger for us comfortable people is more likely that we will settle for less than the Good Father wants to give us or, alternatively, simply drift away from his love. That is where *hope* comes in.

In their time of persecution, the writer to the Hebrews had an answer for the early Christians who were tempted to shrink back or drift away. It was not "seize the day" but "seize the hope"—hope found in Jesus. Hope

1. *Merriam-Webster*, s.v. "liminal," https://www.merriam-webster.com/dictionary/liminal.

is a powerful emotion with a future focus that enables us to persevere, despite the odds. It is much more than the kind of wishful thinking we display when we say, "I hope it doesn't rain tomorrow on our picnic." Hope must be anchored in something; it must have a secure basis in the past and the present so as to confidently face forward into the future. Our hope in Jesus is based on his words and work in his past earthly life; in the present, because he is interceding for us in the very heart of the heavenlies. For the future, the promise that he will return in triumph undergirds our hope, helping us face whatever comes, knowing his justice and renewing of creation will right all wrongs.

Hope enables us to inhabit the Good Father's love while recognizing we wait with a very real tension for the finale. The apostle Paul acknowledges our part in this tension when he declares in his letter to the Romans that all creation is groaning inwardly as it waits in eager expectation for the full freedom and glory of God's children (Rom 8:18–25). Looking at our world, looking at ourselves, we certainly experience this groaning, so in the midst of the tension, we must hold onto the source of our hope. Hope not only helps us wait, it builds our reliance on Jesus and enables us to continue functioning creatively, in freedom.

Because I am not good at waiting, I have recently been using the season of Advent leading up to December 25 each year to practice patience in the midst of anticipation. Of course, as a child I was waiting at that time of year for Christmas presents to appear and the summer holidays to begin (in January, in our southern hemisphere). Now I endeavor to enter into and learn from the kind of waiting the Hebrew people knew in the first Advent, longing for their liberating Messiah to come. Our waiting is for the second Advent when Jesus will be revealed in power, but it is like theirs: expectant in hope yet taken by surprise at how it is working out. We are not in control and certainly not part of the planning. It will be totally God's doing when he brings all things together in his generous and creative love. But certainly worth waiting for!

PAST AND PRESENT GIVE HOPE FOR THE FUTURE

There are two ways the writer to the Hebrews assures us in this Bible passage that hope centered in Jesus is a secure anchor (Heb 6:17–20). Firstly, our previous experience as beneficiaries of God's promises confirms he does not lie. God is holy, God is good, all the time! We have known the relief of being adopted as a son or daughter, of being an heir of the Good Father. As the Hebrews were often encouraged to rehearse through the psalms, God's past rescues give us confidence for the future. We can look back to the moment when we first discovered the Good Father's love and feel again what it is like to be truly seen and accepted. Seizing our hope holds onto that memory.

The writer in Heb 6 then gives us another picture to strengthen our hope in Jesus. Two Gospel writers (Mark 15:38, Matt 27:51) record how, at the moment when Jesus breathed his last, the Jerusalem temple curtain closing off the holy of holies to all except the high priest, was suddenly torn from top to bottom, displaying the open access now possible to the holy God and his promised forgiveness. Jesus our High Priest has gone into that holy of holies to make sacrifice for us, so we have ongoing access to the holy God. That past and present reality builds our hope.

How do we nurture this hope? How do we hold onto this anchor? By continuing to make room in our lives for the relationship God offers. As we have seen, this is not about keeping rules but putting in place the habits and rhythms to safeguard time spent with our Good Father.

Good habits and rhythms make a good marriage too. Even when we have come excitedly with love and respect into a lifelong partnership, we know the wedding day is only the beginning. We must commit to the relationship, guard it! If a behavior or attitude seems to be undermining connection between the couple, it must be reassessed; if life is being lived too fast or too separately, something has to change. This is the commitment the two parties make to each other. So, too, with our Good Father.

Unfortunately, in some marriages one in the couple is not sure of the other's commitment and feel they are walking on eggshells. It should not be that way, so here our analogy breaks down because God is absolutely dependable. We can trust his unconditional love and acceptance and base our whole life on it. Keeping ourselves open to that ongoing love, anchoring ourselves in Jesus, is our part so we do not drift away.

LIVING WITH PURPOSE

To conclude this book's call to come home to God and live forever in the Good Father's abundant love, I have three suggestions. These are not choices between *mind* or *feelings*, or between *spiritual* or *physical*, but ways to flourish because there is so much available from our Creator that can enhance our lives as we, too, love and serve people in the real world.

Make a Difference Where God Has Put You

Nehemiah is one of my favorite Old Testament characters. A Hebrew taken away from Israel into exile in Persia, he nevertheless reached a high position in the employ of the Persian king. One day, hearing from arriving refugees about the desperate situation of the people left behind in his home country, he was greatly disturbed and fasted and prayed earnestly, seeking God's help to do something about it. Some months later, on an occasion that could have cost him his job if not his life, sadness about his people's dilemma overcame him in the presence of the king, and he was asked to explain himself. Nehemiah records, "Then I prayed to the God of heaven, and I answered the king" (Neh 2:4–5).

The answer to that in-the-moment prayer saved his life and that of many others, but the dates Nehemiah gives suggest he had used the time between hearing the distressing news from the refugees until the fateful day in the presence of the king, to prepare prayerfully and ambitiously for a rescue mission. In the moment of challenge, he was immediately able to present to the king a well-thought-out crisis plan. And the king gave him what he requested—permission to lead a strategic journey back home, plus supplies and people to go with him.

The following chapters of his book again show Nehemiah, in the face of opposition by enemies of his people, continuing to be a skilled and compassionate leader. He oversaw the rebuilding of the walls of the capital city to give people safety by bravely involving himself in the physical work and finding ways to encourage others to work hard and fearlessly too. As the walls were rebuilt and new gates installed, the people involved had a very real sense of new hope because God was with them, leading them through Nehemiah.

Similarly, the Old Testament records the story of a young Jewish woman who by winning the king's favor in a beauty contest was able to save her people from genocide. Though now queen, it was not at first clear how she could respond to the threat to the lives of her people, but her uncle urges her to take a risk, saying, "Who knows but that you have come to your royal position for such a time as this?" (Esth 4:14). Esther seized the opportunity to make a difference where God had put her. We can do that too.

Use All the Good Father's Resources

Coming home to the Good Father opens to us all the wisdom and knowledge of the Creator. It gives us a new perspective from which to view good and evil, to see what matters most in life and how human beings are meant to function to achieve their God-created potential. As recovering prodigals or older sons gradually taking on the character of God, we have access to these riches, including the power and authority with which the Spirit endows us. We do not need to feel impotent in a world over which we are commissioned to be God's agents.

Power in itself is not bad. Power that exploits, that oppresses, that imposes its own demands is obviously destructive. We need no further evidence of that than the last one hundred years. But there is a power that is creative. It was by such power that God spoke the world into being at the beginning. We see the creative power of love through Mother Teresa and in less dramatic ways through other caregivers. Among our own families and friends, the power of someone's belief in them can encourage them to make another attempt to overcome failure. Creative power serves as it leads, risking resistance and criticism by initiating change. It is humble power under control, power for the other's good.

Again, we have a model. In the Gospels, we see Jesus—God's way of being human, and the human way of being divine—in perfect communion with his Father, acting with power and authority to bring healing and love to a needy world. His power is not coercive but born of compassion and humility. He heals people, commands the winds and waves, attracts followers, teaches persuasively, challenges the corrupt leaders of his day. As we see the needs around us, we, too, long for this kind of power because following Jesus encourages us to make a difference. Indeed, we are heirs of the Father, growing daily more like Jesus, and equipped with the resources in his family of our sisters and brothers.

Power is entrusted to us so we can be God's creative agents in this world. That power may be needed for a grand struggle with evil or simply to overcome personal lethargy. Whatever it involves, it will be personally satisfying to act in full heritage as God's sons and daughters, to be all we were meant to be.

Listen for the Good Father's Voice

Finally, we must keep listening for God's voice. It was that voice that called us home in the beginning. It will continue to guide us into a full life. We do not always hear God's voice clearly in the midst of life, even though we are his children. Recognizing his voice is learned from experience and hearing, reinforced through obeying. We must be like those sheep who know and respond to their shepherd's voice (John 10:2–4, 14).

Three friends have recently recounted their very different stories of hearing and obeying God's voice. The first is well practiced in hearing God's voice in daily life. She is a compassionate person and often responds personally to need when she sees it. One day walking home from work she came upon a homeless man pushing his trolley, loaded with his bedding and food. Suddenly many of his belongings fell to the ground. My friend started to cross the road to help him but heard God say urgently, "Go home now!" Her first response was to think, "Are you sure, God?" It was not the kind of thing she expected God to say when she was preparing to help someone. But she knew the voice and obeyed.

As soon as she stopped crossing the road to help the man and again headed for home, he let out a frightening torrent of abuse. She hurried the rest of the way and shut the door. She told this story because it was a contrast to her usual experience. Hearing God's voice was for her often a call to do or participate in something. Here it was the opposite. But she was saved from possible danger by listening to the voice she knew well.

A second friend told a very personal story. He confessed to a pattern of disagreements with his wife, leading him into days of bitterness and isolation. One night in bed, determinedly turning his back to his wife, he heard God say, "Turn over to her." The instruction was repeated several times before he reluctantly obeyed.

Immediately, he felt a well bursting within him that exploded into unexplainable belly laughter. His intense anger dissolved and was replaced by a warm flood of tender love, clearly a gift from a gracious God who brought his rescuing power to this difficult area of his life. Flowing from this one time, he continued to experience an intensified level of tenderness and love for his wife. The previous habit of being caught up in prolonged periods of resentment that had troubled him for years was broken.

The third friend was seeking peace in a desert retreat but found there were loud drums playing in the distance. Longing to get some rest, she waited for the noise to stop, but it went on and on, seemingly calling people through the night air to a gathering of some kind. As she drifted in and out of sleep, not sure if she was awake or not, she suddenly saw a man standing at the entrance of her tent. He had dark, shiny skin and was dressed like a warrior. He said, "They have lost the Ancient Paths." In a sleeplike state, she replied, "Why are you telling me this?" He replied, "Because you are listening."

The following morning, with the incident strongly on her mind, she was deeply disturbed. Before becoming a Christian, she had been involved in the occult, so she questioned whether it was a word from God or, ominously, from elsewhere. Fervently she prayed for this to be made clear to her from Scripture. "Seek the ancient paths" from Jer 6 came immediately to mind.

> Stand at the crossroads and look;
>   ask for the ancient paths,
> ask where the good way is, and walk in it,
>   and you will find rest for your souls.
> (Jer 6:16)

The Holy Spirit impressed on her that, just as the message played on the desert drums resounded far and wide, so over all the earth and throughout human history, God has been calling his children home along the ancient paths of truth and love. He never stops calling his children home because these paths are indeed the only way home, the only way to the heart of God. From that day to now, God's call to come home has been the heart of her message too. It shapes every opportunity she has to speak as she explores what these ancient paths mean in our contemporary world.

In this liminal moment, we, too, must practice hearing and following the Good Father's voice. We grow in understanding and interpreting his ways through experience, interpreted by a growing familiarity with Scripture. And through that familiarity, we notice when we have misheard and willingly change direction because learning to hear God's voice well requires a willingness to obey. We must decide ahead of time that having understood what God is asking, we will do it, no matter the inconvenience or cost. Because we can trust this holy God.

We began many pages ago with a story told by Jesus about a father welcoming home two sons. It turns out as the big picture unfolds, that not only is Jesus the storyteller, he is also the one who makes possible the offer of the

Good Father's love by paying the price for us. Whether we are a prodigal or an older son or both at different times, God the Son is our security for the beginning, the middle, and the end of our earthly journey. Through his life, death, resurrection, and return, Jesus is the hope of every person and all creation. So it is fitting to conclude with one more invitation—the invitation at the heart of this story. Hold fast to the Good Father and live in his abundant love. *Remember who it is inviting you into his presence!*

Bibliography

Bailey, Kenneth. *The Good Shepherd: A Thousand-Year Journey from Psalm 23 to the New Testament*. London: SPCK, 2015. Kindle.

Baird, Julia. *Phosphorescence: A Memoir of Finding Joy When the World Goes Dark*. New York: Random House: 2022.

Barclay, William. *The Gospel of Matthew, Volume 1*. The Daily Study Bible. Rev. ed. Edinburgh: Saint Andrew Press, 1975.

Barton, Ruth Haley. *Strengthening the Soul of Your Leadership: Seeking God in the Crucible of Ministry*. Downers Grove, IL: IVP, 2012.

Bellah, Robert, et al. *Habits of the Heart: Individualism and Commitment in American Life*. Berkeley: University of California Press, 2008.

Benner, David. *The Gift of Being Yourself: The Sacred Call to Self-Discovery*. Downers Grove, IL: IVP, 2015.

Chapman, Gary. *The Five Love Languages: How to Express Heartfelt Commitment to Your Mate*. Chicago: Northfield, 1992.

Cuss, Steve. *The Expectation Gap: The Tiny, Vast Space Between Our Beliefs and Experience of God*. Grand Rapids: Zondervan, 2024.

Dalton, Trent. *Lola in the Mirror*. Australia: HarperCollins, 2023.

Dumont, Adele. *The Pulling*. Brunswick, VIC: Scribe, 2024.

Ellul, Jacques. *The Meaning of the City*. Translated by Dennis Pardee. Grand Rapids: Eerdmans, 1970.

Ending Loneliness Together (2023). *State of the Nation Report: Social Connection in Australia 2023*. https://lonelinessawarenessweek.com.au/wp-content/uploads/2023/08/state-of-nation-social-connection-2023.pdf.

Forsyth, P. T. "Prayer and Its Importunity." *The London Quarterly Review* 110, *Fourth Series* 8 (1908) 1–22.

Foster, Richard J. *Celebration of Discipline: The Path to Spiritual Growth*. New York: HarperCollins, 1978.

———. *Money, Sex and Power*. London: Hodder & Stoughton, 1985.

Gioia, Paul. *Shower of Grace: Songs from a Lifetime*. Mt. Hawthorn Community Church, Western Australia: Paul Gioia, 2001.

Godwin, Roy, and Dave Roberts. *The Grace Outpouring: Becoming a People of Blessing*. 10th anniv. ed. Colorado Springs, CO: Cook, 2017.

Griffiths, Michael. *Cinderella with Amnesia: A Practical Discussion of the Relevance of the Church*. Leicester, UK: IVP, 1975.

Hansen, Collin. *Timothy Keller: His Spiritual and Intellectual Formation.* Grand Rapids: Zondervan, 2023.

Hart, Archibald D. *Me, Myself, and I.* Guildford, UK: Highland, 1992.

Hill, Harriet, et al. *Healing the Wounds of Trauma: How the Church Can Help.* Expanded ed. Philadelphia: American Bible Society, 2016.

Jefferson, Thomas. Letter to Benjamin Rush, Sept. 23, 1800. Manuscript / Mixed Material. The Thomas Jefferson Papers at the Library of Congress, Series 1: General Correspondence, 1651–1827. https://www.loc.gov/item/mtjbib009434/.

Johnson, Alan F. *How I Changed My Mind About Women in Leadership: Compelling Stories from Prominent Evangelicals.* Grand Rapids: Zondervan, 2010.

Keller, Timothy. *Center Church: Doing Balanced Gospel-Centered Ministry in Your City.* Grand Rapids: Zondervan, 2012.

———. *Counterfeit Gods: When the Empty Promises of Love, Money and Power Let You Down.* London: Hodder & Stoughton, 2009.

———. *Making Sense of God: An Invitation to the Sceptical.* London: Hodder & Stoughton, 2016. Kindle.

———. *Preaching: Communicating Faith in an Age of Scepticism.* London: Hodder & Stoughton, 2015.

———. *The Prodigal God: Recovering the Heart of the Christian Faith.* London: Hodder & Stoughton, 2008.

Kelly, Paul. "Comment Column." *The Australian,* Aug. 2, 2023, 11.

Keltner, Dacher. *Awe: The Transformative Power of Everyday Wonder.* London: Penguin, 2023.

Lange, Ernst. *Ten Great Freedoms.* Downers Grove, IL: IVP, 1970.

Lewis, C. S. *The Four Loves.* London: Collins Fontana, 1963.

———. *The Last Battle.* London: HarperCollins, 1956.

———. *Mere Christianity.* London: Collins, 2012.

———. *Readings for Mediation and Reflection.* New York: HarperOne, 1996.

Mackay, Hugh. *The Way We Are: Lessons from a Lifetime of Listening.* Crows Nest, NSW: Allen & Unwin, 2024.

McKnight, Scot. *The Heaven Promise: Engaging the Bible's Truth About Life to Come.* London: Hodder & Stoughton, 2015.

Morton, Kate. *Homecoming.* Crows Nest, NSW: Allen & Unwin, 2023.

Mulholland, M. Robert, Jr., and Ruth Haley Barton. *Invitation to a Journey: A Road Map for Spiritual Formation.* Downers Grove, IL: IVP, 2016.

Ortberg, John. *Steps: A Guide to Transforming Your Life When Willpower Isn't Enough.* Carol Stream, IL: Tyndale Refresh, 2025.

Packer, J. I. *Knowing God.* London: Hodder & Stoughton, 2005.

Percy, Walker. *The Message in the Bottle.* New York: Farrar, Straus & Giroux, 1975.

Peterson, Eugene H. *The Contemplative Pastor: Returning to the Art of Spiritual Direction.* Carol Stream, IL: Word, 1989.

———. *Praying with the Psalms: A Year of Daily Prayers and Reflections on the Words of David.* San Francisco: HarperOne, 1993.

———. *This Hallelujah Banquet: How the End of What We Were Reveals Who We Can Be.* Colorado Springs, CO: Waterbrook, 2021.

Piper, John. *Desiring God: Meditations of a Christian Hedonist.* Portland, OR: Multnomah, 1986.

Sanford, Agnes. *The Healing Light.* Rev. ed. New York: Ballantine, 1972.

Sheridan, Greg. *How Christians Can Succeed Today: Reclaiming the Genius of the Early Church*. Crows Nest, NSW: Allen & Unwin, 2025.
Smail, Thomas A. *The Forgotten Father: Rediscovering the Heart of the Christian Gospel* London: Hodder & Stoughton, 1980.
Smedes, Lewis B. *Shame and Grace: Healing the Shame We Don't Deserve*. Grand Rapids: Zondervan, 1993.
Smith, James Bryan. *The Good and Beautiful God: Falling in Love with the God Jesus Knows*. London: Hodder & Stoughton, 2010.
Smith, Mandy. *Confessions of an Amateur Saint: The Christian Leader's Journey from Self-Sufficiency to Reliance on God*. Colorado Springs, CO: NavPress, 2024.
Stark, Rodney. *The Rise of Christianity: How the Obscure, Marginal Jesus Movement Became the Dominant Religious Force in the Western World in a Few Centuries*. San Francisco: HarperSanFrancisco, 1996.
Stevens, Paul R. *The Equipper's Guide to Every-Member Ministry*. Downers Grove, IL: IVP, 1992.
Stott, John. *The Message of Ephesians: God's New Society*. The Bible Speaks Today. Nottingham, UK: IVP, 2009.
———. *The Message of the Sermon on the Mount: Christian Counter-Culture*. Leicester, UK: IVP, 1978.
Thielicke, Helmut. *The Waiting Father: Sermons on the Parables of Jesus*. Translated by John W. Doberstein. London: James Clarke, 1959.
Tournier, Paul. *A Place for You*. Translated by Edwin Hudson. London: SCM, 1968.
Turner, Jennifer. *Finding Your Voice: Engaging Confidently in All God Created You to Be*. Eugene, OR: Resource, 2021.
———. "He Gives His People Rest." *Zadok Perspectives* 16 (1986) 6.
———. "The Hunger for Intimacy." *Zadok Perspectives* 32 (1990) 15.
———. "Paradise a City?" *Zadok Perspectives* 11 (1985) 7.
———. "Theology of Everyday Life." In *Vose Seminary at 50*, edited by Nathan Hobby et al., 212–17. Preston, VIC: Mosaic, 2013.
———. "Turning Points in Contemplative Life: Uncovering the Healing Power of Awe." *The Stitt Oration* 2023, The Dayspring Community. https://www.dayspring.org.au/the-stitt-oration/2023-stitt-oration-uncovering-the-healing-power-of-awe-the-revd-dr-jennifer-turner-oam#/.
Willard, Dallas. *The Divine Conspiracy: Rediscovering Our Hidden Life in God*. London: HarperCollins, 1998.
———. *The Great Omission: Reclaiming Jesus's Essential Teachings on Discipleship*. San Francisco: Harper, 2006.
———. *Renovation of the Heart: Putting on the Character of Christ*. Colorado Springs, CO: NavPress, 2002. Kindle.
———. *The Spirit of the Disciplines: Understanding How God Changes Lives*. New York: Harper Collins, 1991.
Wink, Walter. *Powers That Be*. New York: Doubleday, 1998.
Wright, N. T. *Surprised by Hope: Original, Provocative and Practical*. London: SPCK, 2007. Kindle.
Wright, N. T., and Michael Bird. *Jesus and the Powers: Christian Political Witness in an Age of Totalitarian Terror and Dysfunctional Democracies*. London: SPCK, 2024.

www.ingramcontent.com/pod-product-compliance
Lightning Source LLC
LaVergne TN
LVHW050647100826
845148LV00011B/2021
* 9 7 9 8 3 8 5 2 6 7 9 6 5 *